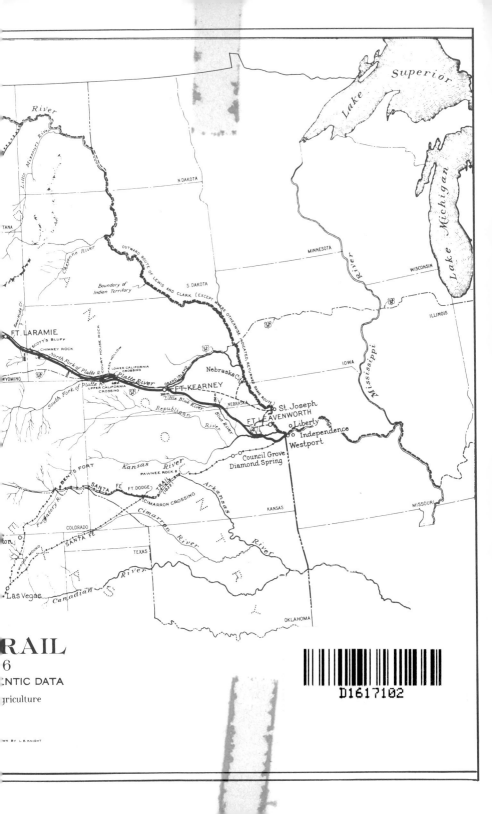

Lake Superior

Lake Michigan

River

Little Missouri River

Cheyenne River

MONTANA

N DAKOTA

MINNESOTA

WISCONSIN

ILLINOIS

OUTWARD ROUTE OF LEWIS AND CLARK (EXCEPT WHERE OTHERWISE INDICATED RETURN AND SAME ROUTE)

Boundary of Indian Territory

S DAKOTA

IOWA

Mississippi River

FT. LARAMIE
SCOTT'S BLUFF
CHIMNEY ROCK
North Fork of Platte River
COURT HOUSE ROCK
ASH HOLLOW
LOWER CALIFORNIA CROSSING

WYOMING

South Fork of Platte R.
UPPER CALIFORNIA CROSSING

Platte River

GRAND ISLAND

FT. KEARNEY

Nebraska City

NEBRASKA

Little Blue River

Republican

Blue River

St. Joseph

FT. LEAVENWORTH

Liberty

Independence

Westport

BENT'S FORT

Kansas River

PAWNEE ROCK

Council Grove
Diamond Spring

SANTA FE   FT DODGE

TRAIL (1822)

Arkansas River

Purgatory R.

COLORADO

CIMARRON CROSSING

Cimarron River

KANSAS

MISSOURI

SANTA FE

TEXAS

WAGON MOUND

River

Las Vegas   Canadian   River

OKLAHOMA

RAIL
6
NTIC DATA

griculture

WN BY L.E.KNIGHT

DESTINATION, WEST!

Destination, West!

A Pioneer Woman on the Oregon Trail

By

AGNES RUTH SENGSTACKEN

BINFORDS & MORT, *Publishers*

2505 S. E. 11th Avenue   Portland, Oregon 97242

Destination, West!

LIBRARY OF CONGRESS CATALOG CARD NUMBER: 72-87307
ISBN: 0-8323-0207-4

Printed in the United States of America

SECOND EDITION

DESTINATION, WEST!

CHAPTER ONE

THIS is my mother's true life story. It is the record of a long and eventful life lived in the remote and primitive Coos country of Oregon Territory. My mother thinks it may be a trifle egotistical for her to tell this simple, human story of her experiences. She says thousands of other pioneer women had practically the same experiences, many of them far more exciting and interesting than hers. Perhaps this is true. But they did not record them and now they are irrevocably lost and gone.

Therefore, this story of my mother's is the simple history of a pioneer woman and other women like her. It is a way of life that has vanished forever from the American scene.

This is her story.

I WAS born in Thompkins County, Ulysses Township, State of New York, on January 13, 1825. I was next to the youngest in a family of nine children. My parents were Peter and Elizabeth Mead Selover. I was named "Esther Mehitable", for my two grandmothers. I do not remember my maternal grandmother, Esther Pelton, but I have a vivid recollection of my paternal grandmother, Mehitable Letts, who lived with us when I was a small child. She was a little, wrinkled old lady of ninety-five years, alert and active physically, but inclined to be forgetful. My father's family had been among the earliest Dutch settlers of New Jersey, and my mother's among the earliest English settlers of New York. My mother was born in the city of New York, in 1787, and my father three years earlier, in the same state.

A distant relative of mine, delving into the annals of the past, says that the Selovers came originally from France, where the name was spelled "Selovier". They fled from their native land to escape religious persecution, locating in Holland, where the name was corrupted to its present form, thus obliterating all trace of its French origin.

My childhood home was situated between Lake Cayuga and Lake Seneca, in a part of New York state noted for its scenic beauty. Our house was a mile away from lovely Lake Cayuga, and our land sloped gently down to its crystal blue waters.

Some of my happiest recollections of those early years are of going down to the lake with my brothers and sisters to wade and frolic in its clear, calm shallows, or to ride over its usually placid surface in a small boat we children owned.

My father had three large boats that carried passengers and freight to different parts of the lake, but I do not think he spent much time on them, though he was frequently absent from home.

Another one of my vivid childhood recollections not so pleasant as that just mentioned concerned Walter, one of my father's hired men. Walter had been with my father for years and was treated as one of the family. As I recall the incident, he had just returned from a visit to New York City, which at that time was experiencing a mild epidemic of smallpox. One evening we were all seated in our big, old-fashioned sitting-room and Walter was holding my little sister Helen, two years younger than I, on his lap. We were listening with rapt attention to Walter's enthralling story of life in the great metropolis. As Walter continued with his interesting narrative my father entered the room. He glanced smilingly about at the happy little circle. His gaze wandered casually to Walter and then he stopped short, looked at him again more scrutinizingly, and called out in horrified tones, "Good heavens, Walter has the smallpox!"

Immediately all was confusion and alarm in the room. Walter was ordered to get into bed as quickly as possible. My younger brother was sent on horseback to bring an elderly couple, both of whom had had smallpox, and who lived in the neighborhood. Our family moved into another part of the big, rambling old house, occupied at that time by my brother Isaac and his young wife. We remained there for a month or more, living principally on molasses and corn meal, a diet that was then considered efficacious in preventing eruptive diseases. Not one of our family had even a touch of this dread malady, which at that early date was frequently fatal to those contracting it. Vaccination was practically unknown and untried outside of the large cities, and there was great prejudice regarding it in general practice. Every morning and evening my father went near Walter's window and inquired about his condition. The answer was never encouraging. In a short time poor Walter died. His attendants carried his body into the woods and buried him there at dead of night. This circumstance made a profound impression upon my youthful mind. It seemed to haunt me with its stark realism.

The woman who had assisted in caring for Walter came to my mother and begged for the bed and bedding from his room. My mother hesitated to give her these things for fear of contagion. But the poor woman pleaded hard for them and promised that she would wash them thoroughly in the running stream in the forest and would then leave them in the sunshine until all possibility of contagion was gone. At last, my mother gave a reluctant consent. The couple departed, eager to be reunited with their married daughter and their little granddaughter. They bathed their bodies in the swift creek in the deep woods, put on the fresh, clean clothing their daughter had left there for them, and then took their homeward way. But they had neglected one great essential to safety: they had omitted to wash their heads. The little grandchild saw them coming. She ran to meet them and was caught up in their outstretched arms. She soon contracted smallpox, dying soon thereafter. This sad story was one of my keenest childish sorrows. I shed many tears over the fate of this lovely little girl.

We did not move back into our former family quarters for a month or more following Walter's death. Everything in that part of the house had been thoroughly cleaned and renovated. I remember that much whitewashing was also done about the premises. I recall that when we moved back great bunches of dried onions were suspended from the ceilings and the windows. These were popularly supposed to act as a disinfectant, absorbing a contagion, or germs, as we would call them now, and purifying the air. The windows were left wide open day and night and the fresh air and the bright sunshine streamed into the house. After we returned to our quarters, the windows were usually closed, as the pioneers were inclined to consider the night air injurious.

I do not remember how many rooms our house contained, but I know that it was very large. It seemed to be always full of guests, many of whom my father brought home with him. My mother was a past mistress in the art of story-telling and she would hold us spellbound by her side indefinitely as she related interesting tales of her childhood and youth. One of her stories that perhaps impressed me most—I was a child of superstitious mould—was about their "haunted" house. This was a large brick building somewhere in New York City; my mother had no idea just where it was. As the old story runs: one day her parents left their home for a short visit, taking their two little daughters with them. They left the place in charge of their negro servants. While the family was absent, these servants decided to have a grand celebration— a real old-fashioned "darky" dance. Many guests were invited. When the party was in progress all went well as the proverbial marriage bell for a time. But suddenly, in the midst of the festivities, strange sounds were heard. Queer, ominous knocks appeared to come from beneath the floor. At first, little attention was paid to these sounds. The dance still went merrily on. But the strange knocks continued, now seeming to come from the walls and ceiling. The frightened guests looked at each other appealingly. What did it all mean? No one could tell.

Consternation spread throughout the dusky crowd as the uncanny knocks continued and fear increased. Some of the servants ran upstairs and brought down the old family Bible. This was opened and spread upon a table. It is probable that none of those present could read, but they knelt reverently before the holy Book, earnestly beseeching the "Good Lawd" to deliver them from these unholy spirits. Despite all their efforts to banish these evil manifestations, they still continued. Finally, the party became a rout. The guests fled "in most admired disorder."

When the family returned, the place was deserted. My mother would smile when she related this story and say that the knocks were doubtless made by some disgruntled uninvited guest. There were many other strange and pseudo-superstitious happenings that my mother told us about, but she always ended by saying that these were not actually true, but were merely the delusions of some disordered imagination. Apparently, however, the owners themselves placed some credence in the story that the place was haunted, for when my mother was nine years old they abandoned it, for this same strange reason.

Then there was the intriguing tale of Uncle William Selover's wife, Hannah. This story always fascinated me. The neighbors called Aunt Hannah a "witch." This was a serious accusation to bring against a person in those days, for sometimes it meant death for the accused. Aunt Hannah knew that these unjust stories were circulated concerning her and she grieved over them. Among other trifling and foolish things, the neighbors declared that she "bewitched" their cows, so that they would not "let down" their milk. This was one of the old accusations brought against many good women in the days of the Salem witchcraft persecution. There was nothing poor Aunt Hannah could do about all this. The unkind neighbors also declared that Aunt Hannah put her children to bed early in the evening and they slept soundly until morning, not once waking during the night.

They were too ignorant and prejudiced to perceive that Aunt Hannah's children were normal and healthy, as all little people should be. They said her baby's cradle rocked when no one was near it. These were all grievous sins, apparently. Many other tales regarding her witchcraft were circulated, but eventually poor, slandered Aunt Hannah lived them all down and was completely vindicated by her former uncharitable neighbors. Yet, after all, Aunt Hannah did seem to possess an unusual gift, that of seeing into the future, at least, to a certain degree. I remember that my mother told us of a time when my father was absent and Aunt Hannah was visiting at our house. One day she asked my mother if she intended making for supper the cornmeal pudding of which my father was extremely fond.

My mother answered: "Oh, no! Peter will not be home until tomorrow. That will be soon enough to make it!"

"He will be home tonight," Aunt Hannah said firmly. "He is coming right along. I can see him on the ferry now!"

My mother was so impressed with Aunt Hannah's words that she actually made the cornmeal pudding, and, believe it or not, "Peter" was there to partake of it that evening.

There had been a romantic but rather sad interlude in my little mother's life before she married my father, Peter Selover. Her sister, Jane, had been engaged to marry young David Farnsworth, whom she had known from childhood. One day David and Jane had a somewhat stormy quarrel, as lovers everywhere and in all times are liable to have. Jane had a quick temper, and it is not improbable that David had the same. In the midst of their argument, just as Jane was vehemently declaring, "I won't marry you, David Farnsworth, I tell you I won't!", little Betsy entered the room. She stood there appalled and frightened by Jane's sudden outburst. David endeavored to pacify her, but to no avail. Again she declared, "I won't marry you, David Farnsworth! I tell you again I will not!"

Finally, David turned slowly to leave the room. As he neared the door, he saw little Betsy standing there, her blue eyes wide with astonishment and fright. He paused before the shrinking child. Suddenly, he said to Jane, "Well, never mind! You'll marry me, won't you, Betsy?"

Fifteen-year-old Betsy replied that she would, and she kept her word. Poor Jane was most unhappy over this turn of affairs, but she was too proud to surrender before it was too late. David and Betsy were married, but within a year and a half after his wedding day, young David died, leaving

Mistress Betsy an attractive widow of less than seventeen years. Betsy, with her infant daughter, Jane, went home for a while to live with her parents. "Little Jane," as she was called, soon became the object of her Aunt Jane's tender love and devotion. Jane declared that the child should have been hers, the daughter of the man she had once planned to wed. This affection for Little Jane continued to the close of her Aunt Jane's long and busy life. Every summer my mother "loaned" Little Jane to her aunt, who also claimed her at many other times. My mother never seemed to begrudge her sister the affection and companionship of the child. Perhaps she felt that in this way only could she partially atone for the wrong she had most unwittingly, as a mere child, inflicted upon her sister.

Little Jane was an unusually sweet and lovable character. We all adored her. No one could know her and not love her. To me, she was the typical elder sister—loving, helpful, and sympathetic with all their childish troubles and sorrows.

To this day I think of my half-sister Jane with regretful and loving tears, as the embodiment of all that was finest in womanhood. It was a blessed privilege to know her intimately. Though Aunt Jane later married Azariah Culver, and raised a family of her own, to which she was devoted, she never lost her love for our Little Jane or her deep interest in her niece and namesake.

When I was about eight years old, my father died, after a comparatively brief illness. Then a great change came into our lives. No longer was our big house gay and filled with company. My little mother went about sad faced and quiet and often I discovered her in tears.

Soon she began making regular visits to Ithaca, four miles away, to consult her cousin, a Mr. Pelton, whose first name I do not recall. He was an attorney and had charge of my father's estate. Each Saturday my mother rode over to Ithaca in the family carriage, driven now by my brother, and each time she took one of her three little daughters, Laura, Helen or myself, with her. This short journey was quite an event for us, though my only recollection of these visits is that of ascending the white marble steps at the Pelton home. I recall nothing else of the exterior or the interior, but those steps certainly intrigued me and made an indelible impression upon my youthful mind. I can close my eyes and see them now, after the lapse of these many, many years. Although we children always enjoyed these little journeys to the lovely town of Ithaca, for they meant a pleasant outing and an adventure for us, my mother came away from them looking pale and troubled. Finally, the estate was settled and my mother found, as so many women have done, that there was very little left for herself and her large family. My father had been a very prosperous man, and was what is now known as a "high liver." He had always provided bountifully for his family, and my mother had never known a financial care.

At last, one memorable evening, when I was ten years old, my mother gathered the younger members of the family around her and told us, with considerable emotion, that she had decided to sell our lovely old home on Lake Cayuga and move to Ohio, to the Northwest Territory, or as it was more commonly known, the Western Reserve. My married brother, Isaac, was eager to go. He thought there were fine opportunities in that big new country for strong, ambitious young men. I think he had influenced my mother in making her decision.

Even at this time, I cannot say whether this was a wise move for us or not. Perhaps it was all for the best. While we younger children naturally felt some regret in leaving the only home we had ever known, and one we loved, it really did not make much of an impression upon us. We were only children, after all, and any great change merely meant another series of interesting adventures for us. The novelty and excitement of moving delighted us. My brother told us —and he really believed this—that great advantages would be gained by new settlers in that rather recently opened territory. He said it was considered a rich and beautiful region, and that everybody who moved there was fascinated with it.

So, after the usual delays incident to moving from an old, settled home and community, we were finally started on our memorable western journey, our Great Adventure. Many of my mother's best-loved and most cherished articles were either sold or given to friends to keep for a time, when she could send for them. Only the sturdiest things, and not too many of them, could be transported such a long distance, over rough country roads, such as we would undoubtedly encounter. However, I believe that my mother did take much of her beautiful china with her in the carriage in which she rode. I know she must have suffered agonies in parting from her belongings, some of which had been her mother's. But she uttered no word of complaint. She was not the complaining kind.

I do not remember how long our journey was. Time means little to children. But we must have been several weeks on the way. My sister Jane drove the carriage in which my mother and we younger children rode, while my brothers, Isaac and George, drove the two wagons containing the comparatively few household goods we were able to carry. I distinctly recall that we stopped for a day or two at beautiful Lake Erie, and that we children gathered lovely shells from the shore. These were somewhat different from those we had found around our own Cayuga Lake. Finally, we reached our destination, which was in central Ohio, about one hundred miles from Columbus, the state Capital, and near the picturesque village of Fairfield.

My mother and my brother Isaac bought a tract of land with a big, rambling log house upon it. Later, my brother built a house for himself, on another part of the land. I have no idea how many acres of land we had, but it must have been quite a number. Soon we all settled down to make our permanent home in that strange, new country. Of course we children enjoyed the change, with its unusual surroundings, as children always do, but my mother and older sisters sorely missed the friends and advantages of their old New York home. I can look back now and see that life was very primitive in that little rural community. But gradually, we seemed to settle down into our new way of living. Some of our old New York neighbors, like ourselves seeking greener fields and pastures new, came and settled in our neighborhood. I remember hearing my mother remark, when we had been some time in Ohio, that no matter where one went, one would always find some kind and congenial people. And so it proved with us.

Gradually, we became fond of our new home in the Far West, of the beautiful country in which we were living, though our memory of life in a distant place never grew dim. We children especially enjoyed life in Ohio. There were nearby groves of maple, hickory, beech, black walnut, elm, and other trees. There were clear, flowing streams and bubbling springs with delicious ice-cold water that seemed to us as wonderful as nectar of the gods. Every autumn, when the ripe nuts were falling, we younger members of the family rode out with our brother, and usually some neighbor children, on a "nutting" expedition. At night we returned weary, but happy, our wagon-bed filled to overflowing with butternuts, black walnuts, hickory and hazel nuts. We enjoyed all of these varieties, but we liked the butternuts best of all.

In the long, snowy winter evenings we sat around our great fireplace, with its blazing hardwood logs, cracking nuts, eating rosy-cheeked apples, and drinking delicious home-made cider.

Ah, those were happy days! Only the memory of them is left to me. There were cranberry marshes or bogs near us, too, where we gathered luscious cranberries in great quantities in their season. They found their place in the cold, dark cellar, stored away with forty or fifty mince pies, frozen hard, and to be brought out as needed. There were barrels of apples in that dim cellar, as well as much sausage and many other delectable things I do not now recall. My mother was a good provider, as well as a very thrifty one. While she had said that there was not much left for her and her family after my father's death, there always seemed to be plenty of everything for us all. My mother did nothing to make any money in all those years, so there must have been some source of income, of which I know nothing.

We became very fond of some of our neighbors who, like ourselves, had come from various old settled communities to make their homes in the wilderness, bringing a breath of the outside world with them. We had the usual pioneer amusements, I suppose, alike in all new settlements. There were spelling-bees, in which the older people often participated. Quilting parties were frequent and popular. Some of the patterns as I can see them now in my mind's eye, were beautiful and intricate. In the long evenings we had our singing schools, in which practically everybody joined. We had many different old-fashioned games played at our young people's parties. We had many lectures. These were very popular and drew audiences from miles around. Of course we had practically no dancing, though some of the more advanced and traveled young people, and these were few, occasionally "tripped the light fantastic" surreptitiously. They had learned this demoralizing practice in some large city they had been fortunate enough to visit. Many persons in our community considered dancing a mortal sin, an unholy and immoral practice that could not be tolerated in their midst. The church people thought that young folk who danced were on the high road to perdition. As almost everybody in the neighborhood belonged to some church, dancing was not popular.

Among other obsolete customs of the past, I recall that we were careful never to allow our fire in the big fireplace, in which most of our family cooking was done, to be completely extinguished. Every evening at bedtime, and this was generally very early, the coals were carefully raked together and a heavy layer of ashes placed over them. In the morning, light kindlings were put on the still live coals, and a cheerful blaze soon followed. If our fire went wholly out, someone had to run to the nearest neighbor's, a mile away, for fresh coals. These were usually brought home in a warming pan, of which he had several. We had no matches, no kerosene, no gas, no electricity, and no coal. My brothers had some sort of flint and iron, or steel, on which they could sometimes strike a spark, but this was a slow process and often unsuccessful.

One of the great events of our quiet lives was the annual visit of the dressmaker, or the seamstress, as she was generally known. Her visits were eagerly anticipated, for she brought with her an atmosphere of the outer world that was both fascinating and refreshing to us.

Miss Drake was an elderly spinster of uncertain age, about which we children were always curious. We thought she seemed as old as our little mother, and she probably was, for my mother was only forty-seven when we moved to Ohio. Miss Drake was an acknowledged authority on all matters of dress. I believe she visited the state Capital, Columbus, every three or four years to note the prevailing "styles" there. These styles did not change much from year to year then, as they do now. What was "good" one year was "good" the next year, and so on as long as it was not shabby or outgrown. Ah, those were the good old days!

There were no ready-made garments then, at least, none in our part of the world. Making a dress or a cloak, all by hand—there were no sewing machines—dressmaking was a slow and laborious piece of work. But most of the seamstresses were artists in their unique way. Their tiny, even stitches were a delight to the eye, and satisfied the most exacting and esthetic tastes.

I recall that my mother and older sisters were busy for days before, and for days after the advent of Miss Drake, getting all the materials ready for her deft fingers to work into lovely creations for us all. I shall always remember the flower-sprigged dimities, the dainty lawns, the muslins, the cambrics, the calicoes, the seersuckers, and the fine linens as well, she made up for us every spring.

With seven girls of varying ages, all eager for new gowns, one can imagine the pleasant flutterings in the breast of each as she listened with raptured ears to Miss Drake's suggestions as to the style to be followed. But there was not much difference in that respect!

We had beautiful changeable taffetas, with many different color combinations, and I felt that I had reached the pinnacle of earthly happiness when I was considered old enough to have one of these really lovely frocks. My older sisters, as well as my mother, who was an exquisite needlewoman, always assisted Miss Drake with her work, endeavoring to complete as many garments as possible while she was still with us. But I remember the great piles of unfinished articles always left for my family to complete.

Our winter outfit was also made by Miss Drake, who came again for two weeks in the early fall. I think our clothes then were quite as handsome as those she made for us in the spring. I have forgotten the names of many of the winter goods, but I recall that merino, which came in soft, lovely shades, was extremely popular for young and old. It seemed to me that we were never without a merino dress. We had some sort of alpaca, and I think broadcloth as well, and of course many other kinds of heavy cloth. Miss Drake also fashioned our cloaks, or pelisses, as they were usually called, if we had outgrown or worn out the ones she had made for us the previous winter.

I can never forget these works of art that came from Miss Drake's skillful hands. These pelisses were quite long, though they rarely came below our dresses, and did not hide the long white pantalettes we younger girls always wore. I remember the beautiful "tippets" we had in the winter, usually made of beaver fur. Our winter hats, or "bonnets," were ordinarily made of a material called "Beaver" which somewhat resembled our present-day felt. It was very glossy, with a long nap and a stiff, unyielding surface. We adored bonnets. I also remember with great affection our summer hats and bonnets. These were usually of Leghorn or fine Milan straw, and were really lovely, trimmed with rich brocaded ribbon, with streamers flowing from the back. Frequently, these bonnets were in "poke" or "scoop" style, with an aureole of artificial flowers framing the young face. These head coverings were almost universally becoming, and we all loved them. Though all of the ribbon used on these hats was of fine quality, I was especially fond of that known as "lutestring." To me, this was like some fairy, gossamer weaving. In those olden days we had no such variety of colors as we have now. All materials were very substantial and of a superior quality. My mother, like most other mothers, selected her goods or materials as the Vicar of Wakefield selected his wife—for wearing qualities.

Although little Miss Drake was no gossip, she always had a store of interesting things to tell us about our somewhat distant neighbors. Like the world today, we were eager to hear it all, and Miss Drake was never averse to telling it all. After one of the little seamstress' visits to our family, I overheard an old lady telling my mother she remembered when Miss Drake was a very pretty young girl—that she had a sweetheart, who had died, and that Miss Drake was so true to his memory that she would never marry, though she had "opportunities." This little biography made a great impression on me. It placed Miss Drake on a sort of pedestal and set her apart from the ordinary beings of this world, with a halo around her head. She once had a lover, *mirabile dictu!*

I never knew what became of Miss Drake after we left Fairfield, but I presume she kept the even tenor of her way until the end, ever faithful, conscientious, and hard-working. When I knew her, she sewed for practically all the families in the neighborhood for miles around. She had her regular customers, or clientele, and each family knew six months in advance just when she would be with them again. After all, there was a certain satisfaction in this arrangement, for everything could be planned accordingly.

In addition to the semi-annual visit of the seamstress, we also had the shoemaker, or cobbler, as he was usually termed. I do not recall that he was ever an actual inmate of our home, as Miss Drake was, but I am inclined to think he was. His visits were as regular as those of Miss Drake. Looking back upon the product of his busy hands, always black and grimy, after these many long years, it seems to me that the shoes he made us never actually wore out. We simply outgrew them, and fortunately in our family with its long array of growing girls, they need not be wholly discarded. I wish I could remember what the cobbler charged for his shoes. I know it was a ridiculously small sum in proportion to the conscientious labor he lavished on them. Not too much attention was paid to making a "perfect fit," but room for expansion was generously provided. Neither have I any recollections as to what Miss Drake charged for her painstaking work, but I am sure that like the cobbler's, it was an insignificant and niggardly wage.

Another important and interesting autumnal event in our family life was the annual candle-making. I can still see my mother and my sisters laboring over this long, slow process. Candles were our main source of light at night, though sometimes we used small, twisted rags set afire in cups or bowls of fat or oil. Many candles were required for the long winter evenings. Though the task of producing these candles was great, the reward seemed even greater. We could hardly have managed to get along without these important adjuncts to our family life. The long rows of glistening white candles gave convincing proof of the ability of the candle-makers. I was always fascinated by this task. It was my delight to be permitted to assist, even though it was merely to stand beside my patient mother and hold the candle-wicking while she twisted and tied it. I think she practically gave up this work when she found a "professional" candle-maker in the nearby village, though she continued to supervise the job to her own satisfaction. Good candle-making really required some proficiency. If the candles were not made a certain way, or of a certain kind of tallow, they would drip or sag or crack, or worst of all, they would burn too fast. I fairly reveled in the long white rows that filled one of our big kitchen shelves.

We youngsters were allowed the privilege of packing them away neatly.

I can close my eyes and see the array of shining copper cooking utensils that hung near the fireplace in our roomy kitchen. To my childish, adoring eyes they looked like gold. There was always an air of warmth and cheer in that dear old kitchen, and small wonder when the fire was never permitted to go out for one single minute during the long winter months. In those icy mornings, and there were plenty of them! it was a joy to leap from our beds to the warm and friendly atmosphere of that kitchen, where the home-made sausage was sizzling over the glowing coals and the big china mugs of hot milk were ready for us children.

Most of our family cooking was done in that great fireplace, though some was also done in the room that was both sitting-room and bedroom. The kitchen was always spotlessly clean, with its white sanded floor and its rows of copper kettles gleaming dimly in the dull winter mornings. Several warming pans hung around our capacious fireplace and these were our only source of warmth during the long, freezing winter nights, with the exception of our thick feather beds, without which I doubt if we could have existed comfortably.

Thus life flowed on quietly and serenely in our new home, which by this time was becoming a real home for us all. But we never forgot our dear old place beside lovely Cayuga Lake, and I think my mother always looked toward it with longing eyes. She hoped that some day she would see it again. But she never did.

Looking back upon my childhood days, I think I must have been something of a "dare-devil," though I am sure my gentle mother never suspected it. One day when I was about twelve years old, I was drawing water from the well when the rope broke, precipitating the heavy wooden bucket, with its bands of iron, down into the deep, dark depths that yawned below me. For a moment or two I stood there transfixed, not knowing just what to do in such a situation. I hesitated to call the family, for I knew they would say I had been careless. I was terrified at what had happened. Fortunately, I was alone. But I could not think what was best for me to do under the circumstances I was in deep perplexity for a brief time. Then a brilliant thought, an inspiration, occurred to me. It seemed a somewhat desperate thing to do, but I could see no other way out of the difficulty. I pulled off my shoes and stockings, took firm hold of the slippery rope, which was probably rotten, bracing my body as much as possible against the brick wall of the well, and with my toes endeavoring to find a hold on the opposite side, I slid downward as slowly as I could to the bottom.

I do not remember what my thoughts were as I slid down into those cavernous depths, but I know that I felt no sense of fear, except the fear of being discovered before I had replaced the bucket. I knew exactly what I would do when I reached the bottom. Still holding tightly to the rope and clinging to the sides of the well, I finally arrived at the bottom and much to by delight, saw the old bucket floating on the top of the water. I had been afraid it had sunk to the bottom; then I would have been powerless to re-capture it, for I could not swim, and the water was deep. After a little delay, the floating bucket constantly eluding my eager hand, for I could use only one for this purpose, I finally caught it, and still bracing myself against the brick walls, I tied it back on the rope and was then ready for my upward climb.

This was a far more difficult feat than descending the well had been. I was not too sure that I could make it. But eventually I started up that long black tunnel, clinging to the rope and digging my bare toes into the crevices of the brick wall as I braced my body against the opposite side. I have no idea how long a time this little journey consumed, but it could not have been very long, though it seemed very long and slow to me. At last I reached the top.

I remember how relieved I was to see the good old world spread out before me, the bright sunshine streaming over it all. It was certainly much better than being down in the bottom of a deep, dark well. I climbed hurriedly out, replaced my shoes and stockings, and was then ready to receive company. But though I waited expectantly, no one appeared. Apparently, the little incident of the fallen bucket had not been noted by any member of the family.

It was not until many years later that I related this story to any one of my relatives. I do not know whether or not they believed me. Perhaps they thought my vivid imagination had carried me away.

About the time of the bucket episode I had another little experience that I thought was quite interesting. We had a young colt in the pasture and he and I became fast friends. I won his friendship first by taking him carrots and apples. Then I would lead him up to the rail fence, take hold of his glossy mane and jump upon his back. We had many a merry canter around that big green pasture, and Jerry seemed to enjoy it as much as I did. But I felt instinctively that my family would not approve of my intimacy with young Jerry, so I never mentioned the matter to them. But Jerry and I continued to have our little journeys together.

The time came when an additional horse was needed for riding to the village on errands. One day I heard my mother expressing regret that she did not have another gentle horse for this purpose. Then I thought the time had come for me to "speak right out in meeting." I remarked that I thought Jerry would be fine for that purpose. But my mother said, "Oh, no, child! Jerry has never been broken!"

"Yes, he has," I answered. "I have been riding him around the pasture for more than a year, and he is very gentle."

My mother was amazed and somewhat alarmed at this, but a little later Jerry himself convinced her that he was safe to ride.

When I was thirteen years old I was as tall as I am now, and the young men in the neighborhood began to pay me some attention. But my wise little mother frowned on these attentions. She said I was "just a little girl" and she never allowed me to go out with any of the would-be admirers unless I was chaperoned either by herself or one of my married sisters. When I was fourteen, she received three offers of marriage for me, but I knew nothing of all this until a few months before my mother passed away. When she finally told me, she added that she had feared it might make me vain if I had known it sooner.

Whenever I see beautiful dishes I think of my mother's lovely china, especially of the exquisite little cup plates she had. If my memory serves me correctly, my mother's cups had no handles, and when the tea or coffee was poured into these cups, they were too hot to hold. Thus the cup plates came into use. The hot beverage was poured from the cup into the saucer to drink, and the dainty, fragile, eggshell cup placed in the tiny cup plate to protect the snowy tablecloth or the table itself from stains or marks. I remember that in New York my mother had told us that some of her lovely china had been among the wedding gifts sent from England for her mother. Some of it had been my mother's own wedding presents. I do not know what became of these beautiful dishes, but I presume that after my mother's death they were divided among my married sisters. How I should love to have even one piece of that adorable china today! I do not suppose there is now a single piece of it in the entire world.

I think sometimes of my mother's old-fashioned garden, with its flowers of olden times. Among the plants growing there, I remember the "love apple," as the tomato was then called. My mother cultivated it for its ornamental appearance only. It was never used for food. It was considered poisonous, and we children were instructed never to taste it.

I distinctly recall that after we moved to Ohio, where we had to get along without some accustomed comforts or luxuries, I occasionally heard my mother sigh and say that if she had her "rights," she would be very wealthy. When my mother and her sister were married, their father, Stephen Mead, gave them each a tract of land consisting of six hundred acres, known as "wild land." This land lay immediately adjacent to the city of New York. My mother was married about 1803 and her sister a few years later. Apparently, little attention was paid to the land the girls had received from their father as a wedding dower. It was probably considered worthless.

Many years later, my mother discovered, in some way about which I know nothing, that this land had been leased for a term of ninety-nine years, according to a custom prevailing at that time. So far as I know, my mother had no idea to whom this land had been leased. Just three months before the expiration of this lease, the "Mead heirs" were advertised for in some eastern newspaper, probably a New York City paper. My mother had then been dead for more than thirty-five years. I was notified of this advertisement by some eastern relative and was asked to contribute in defraying the expenses of someone to go to New York and endeavor to recover the property for the legitimate heirs. This land was not supposed to be a part of the famous Trinity Church property, but it was presumed to lie between that and the East River.

At the time the advertisement appeared, the land was estimated to be worth about twenty million dollars, and it is of course worth many times that sum now. There is no doubt that a portion of the great city of New York stands on this land today. I was of a very skeptical nature, and I had grave doubts about the probability of our being able to recover the land after the long lapse of years. I see my mistake now, when it is too late. I had no money to spend foolishly, so I declined to assist my relatives in their work of recovery. I was far distant from the scene, at that time living in Oregon.

Finally, an elderly relative from San Francisco went to New York in an effort to establish the claims of the Mead heirs to the land. She was making fair progress in doing this, when suddenly it was discovered that a portion of the records relating to this case, had been surreptitiously removed. This ended her investigations. Of course, this was high-handed robbery, a flagrant bit of vandalism and corruption that could not occur in this day and age without a thorough investigation being made and the perpetrators of the crime brought to justice. We were told later that doubtless hundreds of thousands of dollars had been paid by interested parties to keep the claims of the Mead heirs from being substantiated. No doubt this was true. Here, apparently, ended all the rights of the unfortunate "Mead heirs" to establish their claim to their own property.

And now came the greatest blow of my life. When we had been in Ohio about five years, my little mother died. I was fifteen years old at the time. My mother had been delicately reared, and after her marriage to my father, she always had plenty of good domestic help, though she had borne many children. In Ohio it was different. Help was incompetent and difficult to obtain. Unaccustomed to such hardships as life in a primitive, new country presented, my mother weakened under them. She had been a wonderful mother and companion to her children. She had taught them self-respect and self-reliance, as well as respect for the opinions of others. She had taught them to be honest and God-fearing and to follow the principles laid down in the Golden Rule. She had implanted in their hearts and minds a desire for the better things of life, teaching them always to consider the cardinal virtues as the guiding influence of their destinies. I do not think that one of her children ever departed from her wise and helpful teachings.

With my mother gone, life was again changed for us all. I was broken-hearted over her passing, for I had been her almost constant nurse and companion during the six months of serious illness that preceded her death. Three of my sisters were now married and settled near. We had lost our beautiful sister, Evaline, the idol of the family, who had died in childbirth in the first year of her married life. Her untimely and tragic death had been a grievous blow to my mother. After the first shock of my mother's death had passed, I went to live with my sister, Lufanny. Laura was to make her home with sister Eliza, and Helen, the youngest, found a place with sister Jane.

We continued to attend the village school, where I had many interesting associates and experiences. One schoolmate stands out especially clear in my memory. This was Thompson Hildredth, commonly known as "Thomp." He was a handsome, dashing chap, with raven black hair and piercing black eyes. It was whispered that there was a strain of Indian blood in his veins. This may have accounted for his unusual eloquence. Thomp was without exception the quickest-witted person I ever knew. It was practically impossible to pin a joke on him, but he was a past-master in turning a joke on other people. One day in school the teacher reprimanded him mildly for absence from classes and not having perfect lessons. Thomp replied that he had been "otherwise occupied." The grim-faced teacher then asked him to give a detailed account of how he had spent each evening that week. Thomp responded and gave a satisfactory account of each evening except Sunday. The teacher called this omission to his attention. Now, it had happened that on that particular Sunday evening I had passed Thomp and his best girl, whom he afterwards married, as I was coming from a lecture with another girl. We had all merely said "good-evening" and passed on our separate ways.

Thomp started off in his usual grandiloquent manner to tell where he had been and what he had done on that special night. Of course he did not wish to tell that he had been out with his sweetheart, Eunice. Suddenly, he happened to glance over at me. He paused in his long preamble, then said, in a tone that left no doubt of his meaning, "Sunday evening? Well, Esther knows where I was!"

This unexpected denouement fairly staggered me. I blushed to the roots of my hair as all eyes turned in my direction. Later, I reproached Thomp for his insinuation, but he merely smiled in his marvelous way, showing his dazzling white teeth, and passed serenely along.

On another occasion the teacher called him to account. He had again been absent and his lessons were unlearned. Thomp, answering the criticism of his teacher, suavely admitted that he had been remiss. He said he would now atone for that. His nearest seat-mate was one Harris Mead. Thomp rose slowly to the full height of his majestic six feet. He glanced quizzically around the room at his expectant schoolmates. Then he carelessly picked up a book that lay on the desk before him. He opened the book, and turning the pages as he proceeded, he appeared to be reading from it. Instead, he was creating an impromptu rhymed account of how he had passed his time while absent from school. I remember only the first four lines of this clever and remarkable production, delivered by Thomp without the slightest hesitation:

> Thompson Hildrledth gets up to read,
> Right by the side of Harris Mead;
> Thomp will tell how his time was spent,—
> What he did, and where he went.

And thus he continued for several minutes, turning the pages of the book he held as he spoke in perfect rhyme and rhythm. It was really the cleverest impromptu speech I have ever heard. Naturally, in Thomp's extemporaneous "poem" there were numerous sly allusions to the failings and frailties of his schoolmates. Even the teacher did not escape Thomp's biting sarcasm. But he was in a position in which he could not resent them, for to have done so, would have been an admission that he recognized them as intended for himself.

We were all in paroxysms of laughter and wanted to scream at Thomp's witticisms, but the sour face of the teacher somewhat subdued our mirth and prohibited any demonstration.

True to the promise of his youth, Thomp became a locally famous man. He was a minister of the gospel, a popular lecturer and a writer of verse. I have a volume of his poems now, inscribed in his own handwriting, "To My Old Schoolmate."

I continued to live with my sister and attend the village school until I was sixteen years old. Then I was considered sufficiently proficient to teach school. By this time my mother's farm had been sold and the proceeds divided among the various members of the family. Thus I had a little nest-egg laid by for emergencies. For my first village school, some distance from my home, I had keen competition. There was then a slight prejudice to giving the position to a woman, especially if that "woman" was a slender girl of sixteen.

In those good old days women were not popularly supposed to possess the ability or the mental equipment of men. Women were not even considered citizens of this country, even though they were born here. Politically, they were classed with the negroes, the idiots, and the insane. But I won out against my competitors, probably because I was willing to accept a salary of a dollar and a half a week, which was offered me, while my illustrious opponents held out for two dollars. But I was glad to get the school at any salary, for it meant a start in teaching for me, and that was what I wanted. It was customary to pay men teachers more than women because of their supposed mental superiority.

According to the rural custom in vogue, I "boarded round," and had many amusing experiences, as well as many that were far from amusing, such as come to most young teachers. Fortunately, I had a keen sense of humor, otherwise I might have been quite unhappy at times. I continued to teach and then attend school for alternate years until I was nineteen years old. Then I went to Norwalk, a beautiful town near Fairfield, and enrolled as a student in "Miss Flanders Norwalk Academy."

Locally, this was considered the seat of all learning in that neighborhood. I believe that Miss Flanders taught what today might be considered a college course. I had all advanced studies, among them chemistry, French, and botany, all of which I thoroughly enjoyed. Today, I can read my French books and analyze a flower just as I did in those distant days.

I was very happy at this interesting school and enjoyed my work there. It was never any trouble for me to learn my lessons. I had an excellent memory, which always served me well. When I had attended Miss Flanders' Academy for about a year, I was immensely pleased and surprised to have her ask me to become vice-principal, with herself continuing as principal. I accepted this unexpected honor with many misgivings as to my ability to "make good." But I got on splendidly, was considered a good disciplinarian. This was quite an important factor in school management, just as it is today. In addition to my duties as vice-principal of the academy, I continued my studies there until I was twenty-three years of age. Then I decided to take a private school, with one pupil only.

This "pupil" was Freeman Goodwin Lockhart, whom I had known since childhood. His people and mine had been friends in the old New York days, and his family, like my own, had moved to Ohio. "Freme," as he was generally known, was twenty-five years old. I thought him a real Adonis. He had wonderful hazel eyes, dark brown hair, and a fine intellectual countenance. His dark hair was worn rather long in the fashion of that day. It curled up slightly over his ears and around the back of his head, and was extremely becoming. It lent an air of romantic interest to his expressive face. We were married at my sister Lufanny's home in Fairfield one bitter, snowy night in March, 1848.

My wedding gown was of brown taffeta, with a tight-fitting bodice and a full gathered skirt that almost touched the floor. My sleeves were the wide bell sleeves almost universally worn for dress occasions at that time. Underneath these silk sleeves I wore long white lawn undersleeves, elaborately hand-embroidered with turn-back cuffs, also embroidered. Through the buttonholed slits in the cuffs ran a narrow blue lutestring ribbon, which terminated in a bow at the wrist. Thus I carried out, probably unwittingly, the old superstition that a bride must wear "something blue."

The day following the wedding was the "infare," as the wedding reception was called. I seem to remember as well as though it was yesterday, the dinner my sisters set out for the many guests about three o'clock that wintry afternoon. Talk of "groaning tables!" It was a wonder that those tables did not fall down with their weight of good things. There was cold chicken and turkey, ham, and tongue. There were no salads—these were practically unknown in those days—but we had many different kinds of pickles and relishes, and all kinds of preserves and jellies. There was mince, custard, and apple pies, many different kinds of cake, fruit, pound, and the latest and most popular of all, jelly cake. I remember cutting the white bride cake with the old silver knife that had been my mother's.

Speaking of jelly cake reminds me of rather an amusing incident in this connection. Elsie Ann, an intimate friend of ours, had recently been visiting in Columbus, the state capital. While there she attended a fashionable tea, or reception, as such affairs were then usually called. During the course of the afternoon, our friend was somewhat surprised to see on the refreshment table what appeared to be a large plate of griddle cakes, or as they are frequently called, pancakes. Elsie Ann concluded that these were probably some new variety of this popular breakfast dish. However, when this odd-looking concoction was finally served, it proved to be a most delicious cake, made in thin layers, with currant jelly between them.

Upon inquiry, Elsie Ann was told that this was something quite new, called "jelly cake," and extremely popular. Right then and there she decided that soon after reaching home she would make a similar cake, to surprise and delight her family and friends.

After a day of rest at home, Elsie stirred up one of her best cake recipes; of course she was totally ignorant of the very important fact in this connection, that shallow pans or tins had recently been manufactured for the baking of these delectable layer cakes. But ignorance was bliss in her case, even though that bliss was short-lived. Her cake batter finished, she carefully buttered an ordinary cake pan, spread a thin layer of batter over the bottom, then a layer of currant jelly upon this, then another layer of batter, and so on until she had four or five layers of each in the pan, concluding with the cake batter. Then, with a look of supreme satisfaction, and with no misgivings as to the outcome, she placed the precious cake carefully in the oven and with a sigh of relief closed the oven door.

In about twenty minutes, she opened the oven door. To her consternation, she instantly perceived that something had gone awry with her "jelly cake." It had risen in spots and fallen in others. Tiny rivulets of melted jelly ran down the sides of the pan. Here and there, on the surface, little wells of bubbling jelly appeared. Poor Elsie Ann was disappointed and confounded. This was not the jelly cake of her dreams.

Her adventure with the "jelly cake" was for some time an amusing topic among her family and friends, to her great embarrassment. But clever Elsie Ann soon discovered the cause of her failure and ordered a set of the shallow baking pans from her friends in Columbus.

We also had several kinds of home-made wine, among them dandelion, elderberry, and the ever-present and well-liked metheglin, or Mead, made with honey.

After the festivities were over, we set out in Freme's old-fashioned buggy for the little home he had provided for me on the farm he had recently acquired. I thought then that my teaching days were over, but one never knows what the future may bring. I was deeply in love with my handsome magnetic husband and very happy in my new environment. But it was not long before I realized that my husband was not a "born" farmer. He really never enjoyed the work. He did not mind the ploughing, sowing, or reaping, for then he could let his imagination run riot and dream. And he had many dreams, too. When his feet were on the ground, his head was among the stars. Caring for cattle, horses, and swine appealed to him not at all. His tastes were more of the intellectual type, and that does not imply that a farmer can not be intellectual. The life was simply not the one for Freeman. He could not thrive or rise to his highest levels under it.

He gradually gave up much of the farm work and spent most of his time on short trips about the country lecturing for the "Sons of Temperance," a popular organization in our part of the world at that period. Freeman was a convincing speaker and enjoyed this kind of work. Words seemed to fairly flow from his lips. His remarkable vocabulary often amazed me with its rich fluency. Occasionally, I attended one of his lectures and was astonished and interested in the unusual things he frequently did. Freeman had an unusually persuasive personality. I think he had in large degree the quality that we now often describe as "personal magnetism."

After delivering an eloquent and convincing address upon the evils of intemperance, he would frequently call upon anybody in the audience to come forward to the platform and test the so-called power of "mesmerism." This was quite a popular form of entertainment about that time, although not everyone was successful with it. Usually, there were persons present who desired this experience, most of them, naturally, refusing to believe that any other mind could influence theirs.

Ordinarily, Freeman had these unbelievers under his "influence" in a few minutes. He rarely hesitated to use his power on these self-righteous and self-contained individuals who openly scoffed and doubted his ability to mesmerize them. These persons came forward voluntarily, always eager to show the waiting audience how superior their wills were, and to prove that they were invulnerable to all attempts of this nature.

This mesmerism was also known as "mental telepathy," a term that has in later years assumed some importance in psychological experiments. Freeman had spent some time studying all that he could find concerning this mysterious subject and he was really very proficient and clever in its application. I think he would have done well if he had gone farther afield with his rather extraordinary powers. I used to sit in the audience, sometimes trembling nervously and wondering what would happen next and marvelling at Freeman's strange faculty. To me, it seemed almost uncanny, as well as somewhat dangerous to both him and his subjects. But he never permitted it to go beyond a certain safety point, at which he could instantly restore people to their normal condition of mind and body. When he perceived that anyone was becoming too helpless or lapsing too far into unconsciousness, he immediately called him back to realities.

I remember that one evening after the lecture a certain prominent judge, well-known for his strong will, came forward to the platform to show the assembly that he was invulnerable to such childish practices as the audience had just witnessed. Freeman was not inclined to be easy with this man, as he had boasted openly that he would show everybody how little there was in this whole business. Freeman soon found, to his surprise, that the judge was a very easy subject to handle. He first told him to look intently into the operator's eyes. Then he made a few "passes" over the judge's face. He had previously told me that these passes meant nothing, so far as the actual mesmerizing was concerned, but they impressed the subject and the audience and helped to fix the attention of both on the mesmerizer.

In a few minutes it was apparent to all that the strong-willed judge had succumbed completely to the "influence." Freeman made a regular plaything of him. He told the grave and pompous magistrate that he was a negro mammy from away down south. He then put a rag doll into his hands and told him this was his baby. The sedate judge rocked back and forth, fondling and caressing the inanimate object, and crooning old-time darky lullabies. He called it by many endearing names, while the audience fairly roared with amusement. Finally when those present had sufficiently enjoyed this sorry spectacle of the judge acting like a clown, Freeman brought him out of his hypnotic state. When he was told what he had done, he refused to believe it, asserting that he was conscious of what he was doing all the time, and merely acted as he did to show the audience and the mesmerizer how easy it was to deceive people.

Several other unbelievers were also put under the "spell" that evening. It was astonishing how many intelligent people wanted to try this game. I was not altogether pleased with these unusual powers possessed by my husband. I felt that the whole thing was fraught with danger to everybody concerned. I wondered what would happen to persons under control if Freeman were to be taken suddenly ill, or any other serious change should come to him while he was performing with a subject. I was considerably relieved when Freeman gradually ceased to display his unusual mesmeric powers.

As I sit here in my armchair in the evening of life and look back upon the events of my childhood, many interesting thoughts crowd upon me. One is about my sister Laura, two years my senior. Until she was six years old Laura was a healthy, normal child. Then, suddenly one evening, without the slightest warning, she was stricken with a strange malady. She was seated by the fireplace, leaning against the ever-present dye-tub, when my mother called her to come and prepare for bed. But Laura did not move. In a few minutes my mother repeated her command, but still Laura remained seated. Then my mother again requested the child to come to her, and Laura said, in a faint voice, "I can't move!" Startled, my mother sprang to Laura's side and soon discovered that she could neither stand or move. She was put to bed immediately, remaining there for several months until her strength returned sufficiently to permit her to walk with assistance.

But one leg was lame and a trifle shorter than the other, and so remained to the close of her long life. This sudden illness of Laura's occurred in 1829, I believe. My mother never knew what had caused the sudden affliction, as the country doctors she called could give it no name, beyond saying that it was a form of paralysis. Nowadays, it would probably be diagnosed as "infantile paralysis."

And now, I am leaving my childhood memories and my youth behind me forever. I was a married woman, with a married woman's responsibilities.

CHAPTER TWO

IT WAS Christmas Day, 1850, in Ohio. My little house was full to overflowing with relatives who had come from near and far to share the holiday festivities with us. Nobody knew when we would all be together again on another Christmas Day, for Freeman and I, with our year-old daughter, were going far away. It was sometimes difficult for me to realize that we were about to make such a momentous move. But it was actually true. We had decided to go west, to cross the plains to Oregon Territory. It had all come about rather suddenly. Some of our neighbors who had gone to California following the gold rush of '49, had now returned for their families. They offered to lead a large party of emigrants to this new El Dorado, about which they were most enthusiastic. Lecturers went through the countryside telling of the great advantages to be derived from living in the far west. They described the vast mineral wealth of that region, the fine agricultural land, the immense forests of timber, all waiting for settlers to come and help themselves. These itinerant lecturers dwelt at length upon the great freedom of the west as compared with the east. They laid much stress upon the climate there, the long, cool summers and the short, mild winters.

From the first my husband was eager to go. At that time he was twenty-seven years old, with an adventurous, somewhat rebellious spirit that often chafed under the restrictions placed upon the younger men by the stern, staid, old-fashioned settlers of his neighborhood and time. As my brother Isaac had said before he left New York state for Ohio, Freeman declared that there were fine opportunities for strong, willing young men in that great western country. He said he was weary of slaving through the hot summer to save money that must be spent during the long, cold winter that followed. Besides, this would take him away from farming, which he despised.

Freeman had a fine, logical mind and a nimble wit. He would have made a good lawyer. He also had an aptitude for medicine, and his intimate friend, Dr. Bronson, had repeatedly urged him to come into his office and study medicine with him. I believe that my husband would have made a success in either one of these professions. Of course, several years would have been required for him to attain proficiency in these lines, but in the meantime our little farm would have furnished us with a comfortable home and a living. But we had made our decision about going west, and we had no intention of altering it. We were to fare forth into the unknown wilderness with its perils and hardships. Neither one of us had any thought of fear in this connection. We knew, in a dim sort of way, that there were hostile Indians on the plains, who sometimes attacked and murdered emigrants. We had heard of tragic accidents that had occurred, of delays and disappointments, but none of these deterred us. We had no thought of fear from any source. What foolish young optimists we were! Troubles and sorrows might come to others, but we fully believed that we would be immune from them. To us, going to the far west seemed like the entrance to a new world, one of freedom, happiness and prosperity. We thought of our long journey, across the broad plains merely as a great adventure.

Looking back upon it all now, from this long lapse of years, I wonder how we dared to take so revolutionary a step. It was a venture into unknown and unfriendly wilds. Only young people, full of life and health, could attempt it. Older persons would pause and reflect seriously before making such a radical change, even though some of their dearest ones were going into this far-off land. We were eager to be off now. This change seemed to promise everything wonderful for us.

Soon after Christmas, we began settling up our affairs so that we might leave in March. We held the usual auction sale of our belongings. Our farm, our stock and all our other things that could not be transported across the plains were sold, at a great sacrifice, of course. I found it almost heart-breaking to give up many of my cherished possessions, things I had known and loved for years. I thought of my dear mother's feelings when we moved from New York. But it all seemed for the best then. We thought that we were entering into a new and wonderful life, one that would bring us wealth and honors, and fully compensate us for all we were then relinquishing. Pope truly says:

"Hope springs eternal in the human breast;
Man never is, but always to be blest."

And thus it was with us.

Finally, after many vexatious delays, our arrangements were completed and we left our home on March 18th, 1851, bound for a destination more than two thousand miles away. "Fools rush in where angels fear to tread!" I had many a heartache for the dear home and friends we were leaving. Although we had not forgotten our New York days, I had grown to love my adopted state, and to me it was and ever will remain "Dear old Ohio."

My baby daughter was but fifteen months old, and I did not know how she would stand the long, hard journey. My unmarried sister, Laura, had chosen to cast her lot with ours. So I was not entirely alone. At Council Bluffs we were to join a large emigrant company, bound for Oregon Territory.

Many years before this, when I was a little girl in the state of New York, Dr. Elijah White, who afterwards became so prominent a figure in Indian affairs in Oregon Territory, had visited at my mother's home near Ithaca. Dr. White lived in the same county as ourselves. From the day of his visit at our place I never forgot his enthusiasm regarding this distant northwest country, though I am under the impression that at that time he had not seen it. It must have been about the year 1834 when I first saw him. My husband, whose family lived near ours, had also seen and heard Dr. White at the same time that I had, and naturally, we were both anxious to locate in the territory so highly recommended by him.

A hundred miles' travel, mostly by rail, from our home
village of Fairfield, took us to the thriving town of Columbus, the state capital. Here we remained overnight, stopping
at the "Buckeye Hotel," a very pretentious hostelry for those
days. I especially remember that the dining-room waiters
were all shining black negroes. This made quite an impression on us, as colored people were not numerous in the north
in the days preceding the Civil War. Heretofore, the only
negroes with whom we had even a speaking acquaintance,
had been "Uncle Tom" and "Aunt Grace," of our own little
village.

This worthy couple had been brought north by their master years before and freed by him, as he could not believe in
the doctrine of human slavery.Somehow, they had strayed
to Fairfield, and there they had remained, perhaps because
it was remote from the thoroughfares of travel and they felt
safer there. "Uncle Tom" was sober, reliable and industrious.
He served as willing "choreman" for the entire community.
"Aunt Grace" had been a cook in one of the big plantation
mansions "way down south" and her skill in preparing culi-
nary dainties was well known. Sometimes she gave little
"afternoons" to ladies in her neighborhood, and no matter
how high their station or how great their worldly possessions,
no one wished to decline Aunt Grace's invitations. It was
considered a pleasant and unique privilege to sit in her clean-
ly little home, feast on her delicious pies, cakes, preserves
and innumerable other good things and listen to her marvelous tales of real southern life, told in her quaint and original fashion. It was an experience that a northerner in those
olden days would not soon forget. "Uncle Tom" played the
violin, and I fancy he had "fiddled" for many a gay plantation dance or hoe-down in the days of long ago. Sometimes
he would be present at his wife's little tea-parties, and for
the edification of "de quality" he would play some of the
sweet old southern melodies. Probably nowadays they would
be called "negro spirituals." Often, as he sawed away on his
squeaky old instrument, the tears would roll down his

wrinkled cheeks at the memories the strains evoked.

After leaving Columbus, we journeyed another hundred miles, also by rail, to Cincinnati, where, after a short stay at another fine hotel, the name of which I have forgotten, we embarked for St. Louis on the large river steamer *Empire State*. The boat was fitted with accommodations for two hundred cabin passengers and three hundred in the steerage. Though the captain told us that we were to leave immediately, we lay at the dock for four long days, waiting for more passengers. Every few hours the bells would ring and the whistles blow as though we were about to depart, but no actual start was made until the boat was filled to capacity. It must be remembered that the occurrences I am relating took place many, many years ago, and that great changes have come since then. Columbus, Cincinnati, and St. Louis, were all comparatively small towns at that time, and in our wildest flights of imagination we could have hardly pictured their future.

We enjoyed our ride down the broad, majestic Ohio. It was like a pleasant dream to us, utterly different from anything we had experienced before. The word "Ohio" means "beautiful river" in the Iroquois language, and it is truly descriptive of the stream. We floated along its placid surface for days, constantly meeting many other steamers, both large and small. Often our thoughts went back to the shadowy past, when only the Indian canoes or the frail boats of the pious missionaries were on these waters.

We had not been long on the *Empire State* before we discovered another family bound for Oregon Territory, to join the same company as ourselves. Naturally, we were delighted, as Mr. Allen, his wife and little daughter were most congenial people. He was a recent graduate of Oberlin Theological Seminary, and was going west as a missionary. Unfortunately, however, he was in delicate health, and upon reaching Weston, Missouri, he became so ill that he was obliged to abandon his plans, much to his disappointment, as well as ours. It was while we were traveling on the *Empire*

State that we first saw canned fruit. The month was March, and we were astonished to see what appeared to be fresh stewed peaches on the table. The only method of canning them with which we were familiar was the old-fashioned way of preserving them with sugar. Upon inquiry we learned that a process had been discovered the year before by which hot, cooked fruit could be sealed in air-tight cans and kept indefinitely. We thought this was wonderful. The peaches seemed like magical fruit to us, as fresh and delicious as the day they were picked from the tree and cooked. A pretty young girl returning to boarding-school with her chaperon, sat at our table and evidently enjoyed the peaches immensely. After disposing of four large servings, she asked for more, but the steward politely told her they were all gone.

Soon we left the noble Ohio and ascended the Mississippi to St. Louis. Here, much to our regret, we were obliged to leave the *Empire State,* as the water in the river was too low to permit a vessel of her heavy draft to proceed farther. After a few hours' stay in the little city of St. Louis, we re-embarked for St. Joseph on the *Highland Mary,* a much smaller and older boat than the *Empire State.*

One bright, sunshiny day, as we proceeded leisurely up the Missouri, a big white steamer came in sight behind us, and gradually overtook us. This seemed to be more than our captain could stand. He crowded on all steam possible. Soon we realized with dismay that our boat was racing with the big stranger. For several hours the contest continued, both boats urged to their utmost speed.

Some of our women passengers screamed in terror. Others knelt on the decks praying for safety, while still others wept silently. Many of the men swore roundly at the captain, calling him a reckless young fool. Others watched the race excitedly, enjoying every moment of it, and betting on the outcome. It was certainly a time of tense feeling for us all, as we realized only too well what frequently happened to steamboats that indulged in the dangerous practice of racing on the rivers. Our opponent continued to gain on us. Suddenly, the contest was brought to a dramatic close. Our boat, crowded somewhat out of the channel by her formidable rival, ignominiously ran aground on a sand bar! Here we remained helpless and rather despondent, for nine long days, chafing at this unexpected delay. Every twenty-four hours lost now increased the probability of encountering bad weather before we reached our distant destination. Finally, an unusually high tide liberated us, and we went on our way to Weston, Missouri. In those days, this was a place of some importance, for it was there that many of the emigrants "fitted out" for the trip across the plains.

When we reached Weston, the disappointing announcement was made that owing to the low water in the river, the boat could go no further. Therefore we immediately bought a wagon and a yoke of oxen and started overland for St. Joseph. Night found us but half-way there. Seeing a fairly comfortable looking house by the roadside, we asked permission to remain until morning. The motherly-appearing woman that came to the door seemed pleased to have us stay. Almost as soon as we were inside, she told us that she was very lonely and welcomed nice people. She added that she knew we were "nice" as soon as she looked at us. A little later she informed us that her youngest daughter was to be married the following afternoon and that she would like to have us remain for the wedding. She was so exceedingly cordial and her interest in us so genuine and personal, that we were glad to stay.

As soon as supper was over, the daughter, a buxom, sweet-faced girl of sixteen, brought out all the home-made garments of her simple trousseau, and with great pride showed them to me. She told us artlessly that she was to begin housekeeping with six servants, all slaves. Naturally, this did not accord with our strict northern ideas along those lines. But we were her guests, and we realized that it was not our place or province to offer any objections to her arrangements or mode of life, especially when they would have been of no avail. The day following the wedding, the bride and her husband were to ride on horseback to St. Joseph, twenty-five miles away, for a short visit with relatives and friends there. Then they were to go to the groom's plantation, recently left him by his father.

The next day was Sunday, a favorite time for rural weddings in the days of long ago. Hours before the time appointed for the ceremony, which was to occur at two o'clock in the afternoon, the guests began arriving. Some rode on horseback, and others came in roomy, old-fashioned carriages, driven by negro coachmen. We were quite anxious to see the groom, of whom we had heard much, and we were somewhat surprised to find him a beardless, unsophisticated-looking youth of perhaps nineteen years. The bride looked very sweet and attractive in her plain gown of white muslin, and seemed very happy.

After the boyish-appearing minister had asked God's blessing upon the young couple and the assembled guests, we all sat down to a fine dinner, cooked and served in true southern style, with husky young negro girls for waitresses.

The next morning we bade our hospitable hosts farewell and went on to St. Joseph, then a straggling little village whose streets were full of stumps and logs. Here we remained for two weeks, buying our outfit and equipping ourselves in every possible way for our long journey. We bought large quantities of dried beans, peas, bacon, ham, tea, coffee, salt, sugar, wheat and corn meal flour, soda, cream of tartar, crackers, "hard tack," tea, dried apples and peaches, and many, many other things that I do not now recall. Oh, yes, I forgot codfish and molasses! We had to have all these things, and far more, as well. They were actual necessities for this long journey. I remember particularly that we had one large sack of a certain kind of roasted corn, the special name of which I have forgotten. It was delicious, and was taken along by order of the captain, to use in places where no cooking could be done. A woman that I met in St. Joseph, a resident there, gave me a good-sized piece of "everlasting" dough, of which I had never before heard. She explained that every time I made bread I was to save out a small portion of the dough to raise the next "batch." I followed her directions and had good bread all the way across the plains. I was very glad that I had made her acquaintance!

When we finally left St. Joseph, we had two wagons—one for baggage and supplies—six yoke of oxen, two cows and a horse. We fondly hoped, and fully expected, to reach Oregon Territory with all these animals alive and in good condition. Only six of the oxen were to be driven at a time. The cows were to furnish milk and butter for us on the journey, and afterwards form the nucleus for a fine herd in our new home. The horse was to be ridden the entire distance and made useful in rounding up the cattle when breaking camp.

With our heavy loads and slow-going animals, it took us nearly a week to make the journey from St. Joseph to Council Bluffs, where we were to join our company. During that time I had rather an unusual experience; that is, it was unusual for me. The only drinking water obtainable was that in the river. It made both my husband and little daughter violently ill. As our hired man was fully occupied with the baggage wagon, I was obliged to drive the other team of oxen for nearly a week, in addition to caring for my sick family. Our man yoked and unyoked the animals for me morning and evening, and I did the rest. I must have presented a picturesque figure as I walked along the dusty road beside the wagon, brandishing the long whip and shouting loudly, at frequent intervals, "Go long, Tom!" and "Gee Haw, Bill!" Between St. Joseph and Council Bluffs stretched a magnificent section of country, and as we passed along, the settlers on our route begged us to go no further, to remain there among them. They offered us every inducement possible for them to offer. They volunteered to select a tract of the finest agricultural land obtainable if we would only consent to stay. I was delighted with the prospect and urged my husband to remain there. But his heart was still set on Oregon Territory, and no inducement, or temptation, however attractive, could alter his determination. At that time, this part of the country was sparsely settled, but we found the people intelligent and extremely hospitable. We were never permitted to make camp when near a house. Invariably, someone would come out and insist that we spend the night indoors. It seemed as though no matter where we went, we found good, kind friends. There was always somebody to lend a helping hand. It made my lot in leaving my old home and friends less hard when I realized that we had not yet gone beyond the pale of human companionship and sympathy. One night, when we were traveling in southern Iowa, a heavy snowstorm occurred. It was extremely cold, and my baby seemed to feel it, for she cried steadily. A woman living near our camp heard my child's cries. Soon she came out through the snow and insisted that we spend the night indoors with her. We gladly accepted her kind invitation and remained with her delightful family for two nights. These new-found friends proved most congenial people. They also urged us to go no farther west, and as an added inducement to remain among them, they offered me the position of teacher in their local school. But my husband's eyes were still turned to the far west, and all entreaties were of no avail.

We were indeed reluctant to leave these recent acquaintances. But we were obliged now to hasten on our way, for it was nearly time for our train to start "across the plains."

When we were within a mile or so of Council Bluffs, we noticed a man walking briskly toward us. As we reached him, he halted, addressing us by name and saying that we were expected. He then climbed into our wagon and introduced himself as Hiram Smith, our captain.

He gave us all the news concerning his company, told of his arrangements for the trip and his desire to be off soon. He made my heart glad by telling me that his niece, Harriet Buckingham, my old friend and schoolmate at Miss Flanders' Academy, was to make the long journey with us. Her spirit longed for adventure, too, it appeared. This was to be

Mr. Smith's third trip across the plains. Years later Miss Buckingham became Mrs. Samuel A. Clarke, of Salem, Oregon. Mr Clarke was famous as a writer and historian. We found Council Bluffs a tented city, literally, and not a very large one at that. Not a house of any description was to be seen. About a hundred tents and nearly as many covered wagons gave the place a picturesque, if primitive, appearance. Here we remained for a week, waiting for a few belated fellow-travelers, adding to our supplies and trying to get everything in perfect condition before starting into the wilderness. While we waited at Council Bluffs for our captain to conclude his arrangements, I spent some enjoyable time observing the different characters and personalities that came under my immediate notice. The entire scene might have been well described as kaleidoscopic. It was all new and strange, and it thrilled me with its novelty and picturesqueness. A certain glamor of romance hung about this party of Argonauts, going forth valiantly into untried and unknown lands so far away.

They knew not, neither did they seem to care, what adventures awaited them there, but they looked forward with eager anticipation to whatever might befall. It seemed as though all sorts and conditions of people had gathered in that little crude border settlement, all animated by the same purpose, "Destination, West." It was a motley assemblage, indeed. I never tired of watching it, studying it, wondering about it. It fascinated me. Despite the diversity in tastes, temperaments, education and character, there was no friction among the crowd. Everybody was good-natured, though some of the women I met were sad and lonely, grieving for the home and friends they had left and fearful of the uncertain future that lay before them.

As a rule, however, all were satisfied and eager to get started westward. Some, like ourselves, were going because of the opportunities offered them for acquiring wealth and honors. Others, who had suffered from ill health for years, and to whom life had become a burden, expected to regain

health, if not on the journey itself, surely after reaching the
far west, with its reputed mild and healthful climate. Still
others had wearied of the hot, disagreeable summers and the
frigid winters and longed for more congenial climes where
existence might be a little more comfortable with less exertion. Some were actuated merely by the spirit of adventure.
Life was too prosy and tame in their old environments. They
wanted more action, more diversity, more thrilling experiences with man and beast.

I especially enjoyed the evenings, for it was then that the
actual spirit of the company seemed manifested. Campfires
burned cheerily in the darkness, groups of congenial people
sat around the blaze, the men "swapping yarns," the women
usually quiet and serious, sometimes knitting industriously
in the half light, the children hiding and playing in the
gloom before their early bedtime. The sound of many "fid-
dles," banjos, flutes and jewsharps made music on the air.
Occasionally the gay laughter of some happy young people
would ring out between the pauses in the music and the
story-telling and remind us that youth was ever carefree and
light-hearted. The sun beat down fiercely at Council Bluffs
almost every day while we were there, though we had frequent heavy showers of rain.

Our "slatted sunbonnets" were a comfort and a protection
as well. Most persons today probably do not know what a
"slatted" sunbonnet is, for they are among the things of the
past now. For the long, hot, dusty trip across the plains, with
its variable weather, the women were advised to wear sunbonnets. Many of them wore sunbonnets at home, especially
in the rural neighborhoods. The sunbonnet kept the head
from direct exposure to the heat and dust, protected the face
and neck from tan, sunburn and freckles. They were a boon
to women with delicate skin, like my own. These head coverings were by no means beautiful in those days. They were
usually made of gingham or seersucker or other serviceable
materials in some inconspicuous shade of brown or gray,
though many were made of black. Rarely did we see any

bright colors, even on rosy-cheeked young girls. Flaming colors would not have been considered modest then. These sunbonnets came well over the face, the entire front portion being made of a double thickness of cloth which was stitched tightly in strips an inch or less in width and as long as the front part of the bonnet itself. This was ordinarily about eight or ten inches. In these small stitched compartments, always of uniform width, thin strips of light wood were inserted. This made the entire front very pliable, so that it might be folded up between every strip. Naturally, these strips or "slats," were removed when the bonnet was laundered, which was not very often. A cape of the material used for the bonnet extended around the lower portion, thus protecting the neck and the upper part of the back. These old-fashioned sunbonnets may not have been beautiful, but they were a godsend to women on that long journey.

While I do not think we had any fine musicians in our company, we did have many that loved music. One of the favorite songs then, as now, was "Annie Laurie." Apparently, this old song has never lost its popularity. It is probably sung more widely today than it was when we "crossed the plains." It seems to possess a universal appeal. Of course, "Susannah" was very popular. We heard it constantly, with the accompaniment of a "fiddle" or a banjo, and often without either, somebody just caroling it out for sheer joy.

Everybody that crossed the plains or contemplated doing so, seemed to enjoy singing "Susannah." Often the last thing in the evening, before the various groups separated for the night, some woman's voice, perhaps thin and quavering, would be lifted in the strains of some familiar old hymn. Gradually, other voices would join in, and frequently the whole company would be singing in unison. While many of the emigrants were deeply religious, some were indifferent, and others, especially among the men, appeared to have no religious convictions whatever. In a certain sense, they were all adventurers, dissatisfied with their former surroundings, and like Alexander of old, yearned for "more worlds to conquer." As a whole, however, those in our company were a God-fearing, law-abiding people.

Around us were hundreds of Indians, friendly and sociable, and intensely interested in us, our preparations and outfits. These natives were tall, well-formed, and rather fine-looking, known as Omahas. Their ordinary clothing consisted of skins of wild animals, though some of them with great pride disported themselves in discarded garments given them by white travelers who had passed their way. Invariably they were decked out with many ornaments of beads and feathers. They had already learned from their pale-face brothers much that was of no benefit to them. Even little naked children, five or six years old, anxious to display their knowledge of English, would crowd around our wagons, shouting loudly, "Gee Haw! Get up!" but always ending their exclamations with oaths altogether too familiar to us. On and near the Missouri River the Indians that we passed had comfortable houses and fairly-well cultivated farms. The farther west we went, the more uncivilized we found them. They lived mostly in rough, crude wigwams, tepees, or lodges as they were often called, built of bark or branches, curiously woven together. Sometimes these so-called dwellings were sunk quite deep in the ground, for protection against tornadoes, as well as against the cold of winter. Some of the lodges were covered with skins of animals, and usually a skin hung over the opening that served as a door. The love for finery and ornament was innate in them all, and no matter how squalid and filthy their surroundings their bodies were invariably decorated with gay colors and gaudy trinkets. On the first day of May, 1851, we forded the Missouri River and then considered ourselves fairly started on our "trip across the plains." Usually, emigrant companies made an effort to cross the river earlier than this. However, it was decidedly unwise to start later, as large bands of predatory Indians lay in wait to attack any straggling, belated trains. In addition to this danger, grass was poor later in the season and the roads, none too good at best, were naturally rutted and dusty.

Camp life now began in earnest. It proved a little too strenuous for me. For more than ten years I had not experienced a touch of ague, but soon after crossing the Missouri, I was seized with a severe attack of this uncomfortable malady. For three hours I would shake and shiver, then the usual fever would ensue, to be repeated *ad infinitum*. Finally, after taking liberal doses of quinine for a week, the trouble vanished. My, how thankful I was to be rid of it! I actually felt like shouting for joy, I was so relieved.

We had heard much about the hostility of the Indians in that vicinity and were prepared for an attack. A young law student in our company, Tom F. McPatton, thought this was a fine opportunity to play a practical joke upon us. He disguised himself as an Indian by wrapping a red blanket around him and just at dusk one evening he stole quietly into our camp. He was full of life and possessed a keen sense of humor. To him, this was merely a "lark." He carried out the character of a redskin very cleverly. He finally became a little too warlike in his demonstrations and just as we were beginning to feel some alarm, he threw off his blanket and we saw the joke, or rather, the joker.

On Loup Fork, a branch of the Platte River, we passed through a large Pawnee Indian village. The natives appeared friendly and intelligent. A short delay occurred here. The stream was too deep and wide to permit safe fording. As there was no bridge, our men proceeded to cut down trees and construct what they called a "pontoon" bridge, made by fastening the logs together in a long line, or row. On this unique bridge we all crossed safely, though not without considerable trouble, as well as trepidation. Occasionally, while traveling through the fertile region now known as Nebraska, we came again to comfortable homes and farms owned by fine-looking, stalwart Indians. If I remember correctly, these natives were Sioux, and inclined to be very hostile to the whites.

We now began passing through Indian villages frequently. These were both large and small. We met many wandering bands of natives, but they all appeared friendly. Each night they brought to our camp strings of fish, elk, deer or buffalo meat, asking their invariable question "Mi-ka tikeh (You like?) swap." If we saw no Indians, or none came to our camp, we considered it an ominous sign, and our watchmen redoubled their vigilance.

With so large a company as ours, we probably numbered two hundred and fifty persons, and traveling through a desolate country infested with hostile Indians, it was necessary that strict discipline be maintained. Otherwise, the train would gradually have separated into different small parties, thus inviting attack from the ever watchful natives. In the event of a separation few of us, if any, would have reached our destination. Dissensions now began to arise in our midst. Some were unwilling to conform to the rules laid down by those in authority. Two men, well armed, were required to stand guard every night, and when passing through the territory of hostile tribes like the Pawnees, Sioux and Snakes, all able-bodied men were expected to serve as guards. One young man refused to accept the post of duty, declaring that his father had paid cash for his passage to Oregon Territory in a "prairie schooner" and "standing guard" was not included in the contract. However, he was soon brought to terms.

We now traveled for hundreds of miles close beside the North Platte River, over wide, treeless and grassy plains where our cattle kept in fine condition. In many respects the North Platte River is an interesting stream. It waters, or drains, a large territory, but it is shallow and full of dangerous quicksands. In many places it is nearly a mile wide, and only a few inches deep, so shallow that it will not even float a canoe. It looked very beautiful when we first saw it, where it joins the broad Missouri, with here and there a small green island and the great plains stretching away on either side as far as the eye could reach.

As we approached nearer its source it seemed as though we might venture to walk upon it, so thickly was its surface incrusted with sand. But woe to the unfortunate creature that was tempted to set foot upon it! The treacherous quicksands would quickly clutch him in their powerful grasp, and without immediate and very material assistance, he could not hope to escape that deadly foe.

One night, while we were still following the devious course of the North Platte, we camped on a grassy rise of ground with the silvery river flowing serenely along just below us. We slept soundly until nearly morning. Then we were suddenly awakened by a furious storm of wind and rain. Looking out, we discovered to our alarm, that we were on an island, with madly-rushing waters swirling all around us. Immediately, all was confusion in the camp. Women and children were screaming, dogs barking and whining, horses whinnying in fright, cattle bellowing and men shouting orders. It was evident that we were experiencing one of the tornadoes for which that region has since become famous.

Everything that was not securely fastened down blew into the water. All the tents were thrown to the ground. Our blankets, pillows, mattresses, tubs, buckets and tin pans floated away and were rescued with difficulty. Several serious accidents were narrowly averted. The carriage in which Mrs. Williams and her three children rode was overturned and its occupants slightly injured. My sister, my baby and I were in our wagon. Suddenly it was caught by a fierce blast and whirled rapidly down the incline. Just as it was about to plunge into the eddying waters, it was caught and held by several strong men. Later, an old lady who was badly frightened came over to our wagon and asked permission to ride with us for awhile. She said, "It looks like you gals never git scairt. You jest set thar with your sewin' or your knittin' just as though nothin' had happened." Of course we could not refuse her simple request to ride with us for the remainder of the day. Gradually, the high waters receded. The wind calmed down and the sun shone out warm and bright and we partially dried our wet clothing and bedding. Horsemen rode through the water to ascertain its depth. Although it reached the hubs of our wagon wheels, we resumed our journey about two o'clock that afternoon. We could not afford to linger longer than was absolutely necessary.

I presume that some of the good housekeepers of today wonder how and when we did our washing and ironing while we were crossing the plains, with no conveniences whatever. We made no attempt to keep Monday as a regular laundry day, as we did at home. To tell the truth, often we did not know when Monday came. Frequently, I fear, we did our washing on Sunday. Most days were pretty much alike to us and we usually washed when we came to places where we found fresh, clear water. Much of the water we encountered was hard and muddy. So far as ironing was concerned, the least said about that, the better! Naturally, before we left home, we had selected clothing that would not soil easily and which would stand hard, rough usage. We had plenty of sewing and mending to do. We had expected that and had the usual conveniences, or perhaps I should say the inconveniences. It was before we had sewing machines in that part of the world, or in any other part, I believe.

CHAPTER THREE

IT WILL be understood that we were not allowed to travel across the plains in any haphazard manner. No family or individual was permitted to go off alone from the company. We were required to remain together for mutual protection from some common enemy. Thus far, no enemies had been encountered. Things were proceeding smoothly, according to schedule. Naturally, our captain felt a great responsibility for our safety and well-being, and insisted upon strict obedience to his rules and regulations, which were neither rigorous or arduous. Every afternoon sometime between four o'clock and sunset, our caravan was halted wherever we found water, wood and grass. Captain Smith was familiar with the route and knew where to find these three essentials. If no water was to be found at the next stopping-place ahead, we carried some from our last camping grounds in buckets or other large utensils. We did not dare to take any chances on not having water with us. That was the one absolute essential.

Upon reaching a suitable location, determined upon by the captain, the company was ordered to stop. The oxen were unyoked, the wagons drawn up in a circle, or in a double semicircle if it was considered wiser to do this. All the wagons were grouped together as closely as possible.

The loose cattle were allowed to graze until nearly sundown, then they were rounded up and tethered near their owner's wagon. Each family was supposed to cook and eat its meals separately, often sharing some special delicacy with invited friends in the company, for hospitality was not forgotten even in these primitive surroundings.

Thus far, we had suffered no privations in the way of food. Naturally, our diet was not as varied as that to which we had been accustomed. But of course we expected that. From farmers living in Iowa and Missouri, we had bought all the eggs we could carry, about five buckets full, paying

five cents a dozen for them. These eggs lasted us until we
had gone about five hundred miles. We milked our two cows
night and morning, putting some of the milk in a tall tin
churn we had bought in Ohio for this purpose, and every
night we took from the churn a good-sized lump of butter,
formed by the motion of the wagon. This was certainly an
easy way to make butter!

We had a fine little sheet-iron stove, with a tin reflector
on each side. It was wonderfully satisfactory, and cooking
with it was almost a joy. Our evenings were usually spent in
visiting, story-telling or music. Some members of the company had excellent voices, and it seemed as though we could
hardly get settled in a camping place for the night before
somebody would start to sing some familiar old tune in which
practically everybody would join. This always impressed me
as being a sort of hymn of thanks-giving, of praise and grati-
tude for having brought us thus far safely through the lonely
and dangerous wilderness. Our man Williams had a beautiful singing voice and he often entertained us. I remember
only one of his songs now. It was called "Fanny Gray," and
it ran something like this, depicting the jealous sorrow of a
deserted sweetheart after a little lover's quarrel:

> "He's crossed the street, I knew he would,—
> He's gone to Fanny Gray!"

Of course the one ditty we heard most constantly was "Oh
Susannah!" or "Good-bye, Susannah!"

> "Good-bye, Susannah, don't you cry for me,—
> For I'm going out to Oregon
> With my banjo on my knee."

This was especially the song of the younger folks, for there
was a ring and a swing about the melody that caught the ear
and the fancy. There were many variations on this theme,
just as there had been at Council Bluffs. There were old-
fashioned negro melodies that everybody seemed to know
and love. Perhaps the most popular songs of all, however,
were the extremely sentimental ones, of which there were
many in that day. These were always with us. The young

people of today would smile at them, but then they were universally sung and enjoyed. Many of them were very mournful and dwelt on death, especially the untimely passing of some lovely young girl. But there was one song that was never heard. This was "Home, Sweet Home." Nobody could have borne that. Often there would be an entire evening of old-fashioned hymns with which we were all familiar and which seemed to give everybody great comfort. They tended to make us feel that we were not forgotten by our Heavenly Father in our devious wanderings through the vast wilderness.

Usually the women and the children slept in the covered wagons, and the men in tents pitched near, so as to be within easy call should there be an Indian attack, or any other emergency that might arise. Everybody was supposed to rise at daylight, and while the women were preparing breakfast, the men rounded up the cattle, took down the tents, yoked the oxen to the wagons and made everything ready for an immediate start after the morning meal was finished. Not a single minute was wasted at that time of day, for every hour was precious. The team that had been at the head of the caravan the previous day was sent to the rear of the procession, so that all families had equal advantage, or treatment. Probably there were sixty-five or seventy, or possibly more than that, wagons in our train, and hundreds of loose cattle and horses. On this trip Hiram Smith brought out a great number of fine domestic animals to improve the stock in the west. So many years have elapsed since I made that long journey and so varied have been my experiences during that time, that I may have forgotten some of the minor details of the trip. But as a whole, the events of the entire six month's trip are stamped indelibly upon my memory. One might conclude that we were unhappy on the way, longing for the joys and comforts of our distant and peaceful homes, and the dear ones we had left there. But in reality we were very contented. We were young, full of health and hope, and though we knew there were lurking dangers all around us, we did not worry. We took life as it came to us day by day, looking forward, naturally to the time when we would be enormously wealthy and correspondingly happy, through our investments in the wonderful new country to which we were journeying. We were never nervous. Young people in those days did not know the meaning of the word "nerves." We had promised our friends at home that we would return for a visit in five years, and it never occurred to us that we might fail to keep that promise. We felt perfectly confident of the future, of the splendid, beautiful things it held for us. The west seemed to us a sort of Aladdin's lamp, we had only to touch or rub it and all our wishes would be fulfilled speedily. But our promise to return in five years was not kept. As a matter of fact, it was more than thirty years before I returned east for even a brief stay, and then I did not visit in New York state. My husband never went back to his early home.

Life on the plains was a primitive edition of life in town or village. Human nature is the same the world over. Bickerings and jealousies arose just as they would have done in a settlement of the same size. We were all thrown together rather intimately, even though we did not have much in common. In so large a company, gathered from many different sources and walks in life, there was naturally much diversity of thought, interest and culture. Under the primitive conditions existing, it really seems ridiculous that trouble could have arisen over such a trifling matter as mere ceremony, or "etiquette." But it is true that one of the principal causes of difference was over "social equality." Even the formal code of "calling" was not abolished. We were expected to visit our neighbors when we paused for rest. If we did not, we were designated as "high-toned" or "stuck-up." Some of us tried to keep out of these petty squabbles, but we found it difficult to do so. In the company I recall five families that associated together intimately and thoroughly enjoyed each others' companionship. These families were Judge Olney's—Mrs. Olney had been a friend of my old Norwalk principal, Miss Flanders—Hiram Smith's,

E. N. Cooke, Elijah Williams's and our own. Though for many, many years our paths have been widely sundered, as long as memory lasts, I shall look back with keen pleasure to the months we spent together in that wild and practically unknown wilderness. And it was truly a wilderness. We were linked together not only in ties of comradeship and congeniality, but also by the common danger that surrounded us all.

In our company was a certain Methodist minister, a Mr. Allen, brother of the young clergyman who had been obliged to leave us at Weston, because of ill health. All along there had been considerable discussion, for and against, about traveling on Sundays. No decision regarding this matter had yet been reached. Originally, the general desire and intention had been to travel seven days a week, if possible, and thus shorten the time consumed in making the long journey. From the first, Mr. Allen had strenuously objected to the Sunday travel. Finally, the question of resting on the Sabbath was submitted to the entire company. By a large majority vote, it was decided to make no stops except those necessary for repairs, accidents or other unforseen circumstances. As a result of this decision, Mr. Allen, with his wife and children and several other families of the same opinion as himself, withdrew from our company and we saw them no more during the journey. However, it is interesting to know that Allen's party, though resting every Sunday, reached Oregon Territory two weeks earlier than we did, with all their cattle in fine condition, while ours were either starving or dead.

Several times during the journey we met or passed the Powell party, which had started somewhat later than we did and which had a disastrous time with accidents and illness. We were all fortunate about our health, although there was considerable sickness in our midst. Owing to the monotonous and unaccustomed diet, and the extremely unwholesome water we were frequently obliged to use, fevers and dysentery predominated. Fortunately, we escaped the

dreadful scourge of cholera that had attacked the emigrants
of the previous year and also of the year following, when
it was estimated that at least five thousand graves, caused
by that dread malady, were made along the emigrant route.
We tried to observe sanitary precautions as well as we
could, though in those days we did not speak or think of
them as "sanitary!" Then, the word was seldom heard, and
was not used in the wide meaning in which it is now employed. Our captain, Hiram Smith, was a capable, conscientious man and endeavored in every way known to him
to preserve the health of his company. Strangely enough,
our family seemed to possess the only medicine chest in the
company, and consequently, it fell to our lot to "doctor"
almost everybody who was ill or ailing. Our family physician, Dr. Bronson, was an intimate personal friend of ours,
and he had visited us just before we left Ohio, and he had
given us much valuable advice concerning the diseases to
which we would be most liable, and he had suggested the
treatment for them. I might add here that many years
later, Dr. Bronson visited us in Oregon. It was he who
prepared our chest of medicine. Acting on his suggestion,
I bought a copy of "Dr. Beech's Reformed Practice of
Medicine", a new work at that time. By following the
practical, sensible directions given in this book, I am convinced that I have been able to save many lives, not only
while on the plains, but also during my long residence in
isolated parts of Oregon, where I have frequently been
called upon to serve as both physician and nurse. Scores
of babies have come into this world under my ministrations.
The book's strong pasteboard sides, with leather covers, now
tattered and torn, stained by water and hard usage, its
pages yellow with age, was published in 1844. This doctor
book is still one of the dearest books in the world to me.
I think I really value it next to my mother's leather-cov-
ered Bible, which is well over a hundred years old. This
dilapidated volume takes me back to a time that has long
since vanished, when medical men were few and far be-

tween in this new country, and this precious book was physician, counsellor and friend. Its author, Dr. Beech, was one of the first reputable physicians to decry and oppose what was then the almost universal practice of "blood-letting." He also opposed the administration of such large quantities of mercury as was then generally prescribed.

Of course, Dr. Beech, like most reformers, was bitterly assailed by many of his own profession, as well as by many outside of it. But time has justified him. Once when we were moving from one location to another in Oregon Territory, some of our goods fell into the river. Among them was my precious "doctor book," and though we managed to retrieve it, from total destruction, it has ever since borne the marks of that experience.

Naturally, during our long journey with a great variety of persons grouped closely together, many amusing incidents occurred. The little circumstance I am about to relate seemed especially ridiculous to me then. Perhaps now it might only be pathetic. It happened when we had been out on the plains for some time. A certain young man, a good-hearted, kindly-disposed fellow had been very ill with what was called "mountain fever." This disease was altogether too prevalent in our company. It strongly resembled typhoid fever and was a stubborn thing to cure. My husband, who was a natural physician, had "doctored" the boy very successfully. When he was able to get about, he came around to our wagon one day when we had stopped for repairs, and after the usual exchange of commonplaces about his health and the weather, he inquired if I had a "teeth brush." I answered in the affirmative whereupon he said, "Wal, I'd like mightily to borry it offen ye fur a leetle spell. I've got a bad taste in my mouth, and I thought maybe a 'teeth-brush' mought take it away!"

In those days, when I was young and carefree, it was exceedingly difficult for me to refrain from laughing immoderately at anything that amused me. But this time I smothered my laughter and controlled my emotions as

well as I could. I told him in a kindly way that I had only
one tooth brush, and as I could not get another on the
plains I could not afford to lend it. The poor fellow seemed
quite disappointed at his lack of success in borrowing a
"teeth brush." A little later he went to our man Williams
with the same request he had made of me. However,
Williams was not quite as gentle with the invalid as I had
been. Williams was very outspoken in his manner, and he
blurted out loudly, with the addition of some words I must
omit. "Yes, I've got a tooth brush, but I've got only one,
and by hookey it shan't go in anybody's mouth but my own!"
We heard afterwards that the young man had approached
several others, seeking the same favor from each, but curiously enough, he was unable to secure the loan of a "teeth
brush" from anyone.

We were constantly meeting with new experiences, in
many directions. Probably none of these were important
or remarkable, but nevertheless they were all interesting
to us. One of these incidents illustrates the difference in
preparing the same food in different parts of our country.
It is well known that there always has been a great difference between the cookery of the northerners and the
southerners. A little southern woman in our company had
been gradually failing in health. I had watched her with
some concern, as she was bright and attractive and had
two small children. She had lost her appetite completely
for everything that her own larder contained, which was
not a great variety. I saw that she required more delicate
food than she had been taking, so, among some other things
to tempt her capricious appetite, I prepared some dried
codfish in the manner I had always been accustomed to
doing it. I soaked it in water overnight to remove the super-
fluous salt, picked it into tiny bits and made a rich cream
gravy, or sauce, which I poured over the flaked fish and
carried it to her piping hot. When I reached her wagon I
remarked that I had brought her a little codfish, but the
words were hardly out of my mouth before she exclaimed

in a disgusted and disappointed tone, "I hate that nasty stuff! I'm sure I can't swallow it. It makes me sick even to think of it!"

But I insisted that she should taste it just to please me. At last, with a wry face, she took her first mouthful of it, but gingerly indeed.

"Oh," she cried, delightedly, as she actually tasted it, "Is that really codfish, I can't believe it! It is delicious. How did you prepare it? When we cook it in Missouri we leave it in big, yellowish brown chunks, and it is certainly terrible looking stuff. We all despise it and only use it once in awhile because we can't help ourselves. But this is altogether different. You must tell me how to prepare it this way!"

Right there I gave her a lesson in Domestic Science, but we did not call it by that name then.

We constantly saw great herds of buffalo, deer, and antelope, never browsing quietly, or standing still, but always running as though they were being pursued. Apparently, they had already learned to fear man and his belongings. Doubtless they were something the animals could not understand and therefore we were something to be feared and avoided. Occasionally, our men killed some of the animals to provide fresh meat for the party. We found this delicious, with the exception of the buffalo meat, which was too coarse to be relished. The flesh of the antelope was almost as tender as chicken. Sometimes many of our men would go off on a big buffalo hunt, miles away, returning at night loaded down with game. We women always worried when our husbands went off for the day, fearing they might be attacked by prowling redskins. However, as a rule, they never saw an Indian on these trips. Evidently, our men knew where it was safe to venture. People of today would thoroughly enjoy seeing the immense herds of buffalo that we constantly saw. We never ceased to marvel at them, even though they became a common sight to us. They were splendid-looking creatures, great, powerful and dignified, well entitled to be called the "kings of the plains."

Almost every night after leaving the Missouri River, we would hear wolves howling, occasionally too close to the camp for comfort. Their cries were dismal sounds and we always recalled the dreadful stories we had heard of these ferocious creatures when we were children. As we journeyed farther westward, the cries of the wolves were superseded by those of the coyote, close kin of the former. The voices of the coyotes were no more musical or reassuring than those of the wolves, but they were somewhat different in tone and quality. Usually, these disagreeable creatures kept their distance, but occasionally one, perhaps more venturesome or more famished than the others, would get in among our loose cattle. It created havoc until our men and the dogs arrived on the scene and made short work of the daring intruder.

It was while traveling over the broad, grassy, treeless plains of which I have already spoken, that our only fuel consisted of what was called "buffalo chips." These were the droppings of the buffalo, baked into large, flat, odorless cakes by the hot sun. When these were put with light wood kindlings, which we always carried, they burned like straw. Some authorities have declared that if it had not been for these same buffalo chips the crossing of the plains by slow ox-teams could never have been made. It would have been impossible to carry sufficient wood.

The men of our company thoroughly enjoyed hunting, though it did not require much real hunting to find plenty of game. The wide wilderness was full of it, and we were kept well supplied with rabbits, wild turkeys, and sage hens, the latter much like pheasants and very delicious. In all the streams, and up to this time they had been numerous, we found quantities of fine fish. Frequently, after making camp beside some flowing creek or small river, many would get out their hooks and lines and catch enough fish for supper. The only kinds that I now remember by name were trout and catfish, the latter so named because its head resembled a feline's. They were fine eating, though!

John Cheney, the driver of our loose cattle, and Mrs. Olney were the champion anglers of the entire company. It was rather amusing to watch the efforts of Judge Olney to catch some of the finny tribe. He would sit quietly beside his wife, patiently holding his rod or line, but while Mrs. Olney was kept busy removing the fish from her hook and baiting it again, the unlucky Judge never had more than a faint nibble, much to his annoyance. I do not think he caught a single fish on the entire trip.

In many places we found wild peas, which we cooked, and though we might not have considered them so good at home, where we had a variety of other fresh vegetables, we certainly enjoyed them here. Often, too, we came across wild gooseberries, raspberries and yellow and black currants. You can imagine whether we liked them or not, after our long, enforced abstinence from all kinds of fresh fruit.

It really seemed as though the Lord was providing for us as He had done for the children of Israel in the wilderness, and it tended to confirm us more than ever in the belief that we had done right in coming west, even though it was at the cost of pain and sacrifice. Occasionally, we were overtaken by large parties, usually composed mainly of men, bound for California, and all tremendously eager to reach the wonderful gold fields there. Invariably they tried to persuade us to abandon our route and company and go on to California with them. They ridiculed Oregon Territory as a place either for residence or settlement, and described at length the advantages and attractions of life in California. However, I think that very few of these enthusiastic emigrants had ever been so far west before. Though some of our company at different times, did yield to the temptations of these other travelers and deserted us, we never for an instant wavered in regard to our destination. With us, it was still "Where rolls the Oregon."

For some time now we had been traveling through a

very rough country, where there was little level land, though the scenery in many places was inspiring and unusual. We came across great heaps of rock and stone thrown into curious and fantastic forms, and giving mute evidence of terrific volcanic action at some remote period of the world's history. One of the most interesting natural curiosities was "Chimney Rock", an umbrella-shaped mass of stone covering many acres, and having a tall, slender spire that extended into the sky for perhaps two hundred feet. Some of the formations resembled old castles or cathedrals, with broken and falling turrets and pillars. In some places we saw acres of odd blocks or cubes, of a white, porous stone, that looked like burnt bone. In such localities as these there was naturally scant vegetation, perhaps here and there a stunted pine tree or some other shrub that looked almost pathetic in its desolation and lack of vitality.

As a rule we did not stop at any of these barren, rocky wastes, for there was neither grass nor water there, and usually but little fuel. What there was consisted mainly of greasewood, which was difficult to burn when green. Occasionally, however, we were compelled by circumstance to camp for a time at one of these desolate places and we were always glad and thankful to move on again.

"Scott's Bluff" was another well-known landmark on the Oregon trail. It was a huge, irregular mass of stone, about eight hundred feet high, so it was said, situated on the right bank of the Platte River. It was plainly visible for many miles before we reached it and for many miles after we had passed it, standing lonely and majestic in its dreary isolation, and gradually fading from our view.

Soon we reached Fort Laramie, in the present state of Wyoming. Here we paused several hours for necessary repairs. Here, also, some of the company purchased some needed supplies, at almost fabulous prices. Fortunately, we were still well supplied and did not require anything. The Indian agent, who was the sole white resident there, had a comely squaw wife and a family of dusky children.

All through that region we saw a great many Indians. I believe they were Cheyennes and Sioux, and though we had been told that they were very hostile to the whites, we saw no indication of this hostility. They probably knew that we were well-armed and equipped for defense.

All the natives around there were great beggars. They would persistently hang around our camp asking for food and any other thing that caught their fancy. They appeared quite surly when we declined to give them what they wished. Had we done so, we would have deprived ourselves of actual necessities. These natives were thieves, too, and we were obliged to watch our belongings carefully, or we would find them missing. The Indians always had some means of discovering the exact condition of travelers passing through their country. They knew definitely how large each company was, whether or not it was safe to attack it, and just how well-armed it was. As a rule, the Indians were arrant cowards and took few chances on losing their own lives. Often indiscreet persons in different companies would tell visiting natives, who were ostensibly friendly, but who were in reality dangerous spies, the conditions governing or surrounding their trains. This information was exactly what the Indians desired. Being at home, on their own territory, they knew how to take advantage of every mistake or error in judgment made by the white strangers.

Most of the natives in this part of the country had their faces painted and wore their long black hair flowing down their backs, though some of the braves wore their hair in a tight braid. Many of them were dressed in white men's clothing, probably filched from hapless travelers or stolen from graves, which the redskins tore open and desecrated whenever found. Everywhere their one great ambition seemed to be to acquire the white man's attire, and because of this absorbing desire many curious and amusing combinations and costumes were seen. Sometimes a big brave would be robed only in a shirt. Again, another might boast only an old pair of trousers or a faded coat, while still another stalwart fellow

would strut around proudly with only a battered silk hat
perched jauntily on his glossy black hair. We used to have
many a laugh over these queer combinations. As a rule, the
women wore innumerable strings of beads and ornaments on
their necks, arms and legs. Usually their hair was entwined
with bands of gaudy beads, which gave them a fantastic appearance and made them somewhat resemble gypsies or Ori-
ental dancing girls.

At last we came to the famous Sweetwater country and
with relief and delight saw the snowy peaks of the Rockies.
In this region we passed "Independence Rock," another
noted landmark of the old Oregon Trail and the almost
equally well-known "Devil's Gate," which is really one of
nature's most picturesque and interesting works. Here the
mountain seems to have been split asunder, and in the rift,
only a few yards wide, the Sweetwater River, which is in
reality our old friend, the North Platte, dashes in a veritable
torrent through the narrow gorge, hemmed in by gloomy
walls five hundred feet high. I remember that some of us
tried to pick our way cautiously through this dark, narrow
defile, with the turbulent river roaring and dashing near our
feet. Of course we could not go far, but it was a unique experience and somewhat broke the tiresome monotony of our
daily existence. All through this part of the country we found
numerous soda springs. With the aid of citric acid and cream
of tartar, which we had brought with us for this express
purpose, we produced what seemed to us delicious cream
soda. In places the ground was white with alkali for long
distances, and our poor cattle suffered from the lack of
wholesome feed and water.

So gradually had we ascended the Rocky Mountains it
was difficult for us to realize that we were nearly seven
thousand feet above sea level. Unconsciously we had kept
our childish belief that the mountains would tower high up
in the sky, not realizing that we ourselves would be at such
an elevation as to make the great Rocky Mountains seem
very ordinary indeed, as they really did. When the day

finally came when we camped near their base, it was uncomfortably warm, and many of our men clambered up the steep, rocky slopes to where the snow lay thick and dazzling, bringing down buckets full of it. Right then and there, we made ice cream, in primitive fashion, of course, but we all agreed that never before had ice cream tasted half as good.

At last we went over, or through, the South Pass, that celebrated natural road through the Rocky Mountains which, as some writer has truly and beautifully said, "A kindly Providence had planned for that mighty army of peace that was to found a new empire in the far west."

Now, we had crossed the Continental Divide, the "backbone" of the North American continent. We had left the Atlantic side of our country behind us and were now on the longed-for Pacific Slope. We knew that our journey was now half over, and though the novelty of it had not yet entirely worn off, we were glad to see the end in sight. Frequently we saw graves by the roadside, or near it. Usually they were unmarked and were almost indistinguishable from the surrounding region, except upon close scrutiny. They were left in this condition purposely to escape desecration by the Indians, who made a practice of despoiling them. We saw many that had been torn open, either by wolves or savages, and we could not describe adequately the emotions of pain and sorrow that these scenes aroused. At such places we would fervently wish that our journey were safely ended, and we would speculate mournfully over the circumstances that surrounded the death, burial and sacrilege. Of course these were sad, morbid thoughts, but we had little else to think about at such times.

We crossed successively the Little and Big Sandy Rivers, and when we were about twelve hundred miles from Council Bluffs, the families of Hiram Smith and E. N. Cooke left us for Salt Lake City. Mr. Smith took with him four big wagon loads of merchandise to sell to the Mormons. He had already shipped forty thousand dollars' worth of goods around the Horn, bound for the same destination. It would be well-nigh impossible for me to express how deeply we regretted losing these two families and how we missed them continually. Separation from them was really a personal grief, as we had become greatly attached during the long months of our association. Much later, these two families came on to Oregon, where they lived for years, being considered among the most highly respected people in the state. Upon Mr. Smith's departure from our company, Elijah Williams was elected captain, and a very excellent leader he made, too.

In respect to evil happenings, our company was singularly fortunate. Only one tragedy threw its dark shadows over us during the whole trip and that was caused by an accident in our own ranks. Elijah Williams, our newly-elected captain, had with him his wife, three young sons and a little daughter. He had brought his carriage along for the family, and ordinarily they all rode in this vehicle. On this particular day, however, Johnny, a bright lad of ten years, had asked and obtained permission to ride in the baggage wagon with the driver. This was considered quite an adventure by the boys, something not quite as prosy as riding day after day in the more comfortable carriage. Just exactly how the dreadful accident occurred, we never knew definitely. The supposition was that the driver fell asleep, the day being very warm, and that the oxen, finding themselves unguided, took fright and ran away, throwing little Johnny out of the wagon. We were traveling just ahead of Mr. Williams' wagon that day, and as the team ran wildly past us, the driver, his face white with terror, cried out, "I'm afraid Johnny's killed!"

The entire train was immediately stopped. We were the first to reach poor little Johnny, and we saw at once that he was beyond earthly aid. The heavy wagon wheels had passed directly over his forehead and face, and death must have been instantaneous. The innocent victim never knew what had happened to him and when Mr. Williams, who was an extraordinarily devoted father saw the lifeless form of his child he was beside himself with grief and anger. He ran for his gun and was about to shoot the unfortunate driver when four men overpowered him and took his weapon away. Later, when reason and calm judgment returned to the distraught father, he was thankful he had been restrained from committing a heinous crime.

The driver was broken-hearted over the tragedy. He did not recover from the effects of this deplorable accident during the remainder of the journey. A rude casket was improvised from a large trunk belonging to Mrs. Williams, and the body of the dear little lad who had been a merry companion a few hours before, and loved by everybody, was tenderly buried near the scene of the accident. After some hymns had been sung and a few prayers said, a wooden marker was placed at the head of his grave. The parents wished this to be done, as they felt that we were now in a neighborhood where the Indians would not disturb such places. On the headstone was written the little lad's name, his age and the brief circumstances attending his death. Then, with many regretful tears for the promising young life so suddenly and cruelly cut short, we drove sadly away, leaving him alone in the wilderness, in his last long sleep. For many days we could not forget this agonizing experience. It hung over us like a black shadow. It took all the joy out of our lives, it had been so sudden, so unnecessary, so full of all that was sad and tragic.

CHAPTER FOUR

AT Green River, a large and beautiful stream in the present state of Wyoming, we had rather an unpleasant and costly experience, though not an unusual one for emigrants of that period as we discovered afterwards. The Indian agent there, like most of the others we had met along our route, had a dusky wife and a family of half-breed children. He told us it would be dangerous for us to attempt fording the river, as it was deep and full of treacherous holes. However, he offered to ferry us over for ten dollars a team. Of course, all we could do, or at least, thought we could do, was to accept his offer, as we had no wish to risk our lives or those of our stock and also our goods.

The wily agent reaped quite a harvest from our company that day, as nobody in the train attempted to ford. Later, we met a large party of emigrants that had forded the river the same day that the agent had ferried us over. He had told them exactly the same story, but some of their men, rather skeptical of the truth of the agent's assertions, had ridden farther up the stream and had found an excellent place to ford.

I shall always remember Green River as an especially attractive-looking place. The water was of an unusually beautiful shade of green, from which fact the name is derived. The banks were bordered thickly with willows and aspen trees. Somewhere in this region we crossed a desert, twenty-eight miles in extent. I recall that we started over it at four o'clock in the afternoon and traveled all night to escape the heat and the dust. Some rattlesnakes were seen in this locality, and here, too, we saw the first horned toads, curious little creatures the color of the sand. They were perfectly harmless, though they looked forbidding with their long tails and their bodies covered with knobby-looking projections. We captured a few and carried them as pets for quite some time. Finally, they grew languid and drooping and we let them go free again. These little creatures of the wild do not seem to thrive in captivity.

The journey from Green River to Fort Hall, on the Snake River, in the present state of Idaho, was uneventful, though that entire country was infested with hostile savages that had attacked and destroyed several parties of emigrants, or at least, so we had been told. We constantly feared that we might also fall victims to their hatred and fury, but fortunately we escaped attack.

At Fort Hall the Olneys left us to visit a brother of the Judge's, who was an Indian agent at some fort or station near there; I believe it was Walla Walla.

We were now approaching Rock Creek, a tributary of the Snake River, which was considered one of the most dangerous of the entire two thousand-mile journey. We had been warned repeatedly to be on our guard here, as the Indians in that neighborhood were unusually hostile and had attacked many parties camped there at various times. We reached this place about four o'clock one afternoon and were immediately alarmed to find a party of twenty-five or thirty Indians already camped there, their ponies tethered near. However, much to our relief, we soon discovered that they were a friendly band returning from California to their village on the Missouri, under the leadership of Dick, an intelligent half-breed. It is probably due to the presence and assistance of this party that I am able to tell this story now.

Rock Creek was really a beautiful spot. A crystal clear stream, abounding in fine fish, flowed over a rocky bed. Ferns and wild flowers lined the banks, and a grove of willows extended for some distance on both sides of the creek. After making camp our men had been busily engaged in putting their firearms in perfect condition, preparing for the conflict that all feared was about to come. As we had traveled a great distance and had never before required arms for defense, the entire company had been lulled into a feeling of false security regarding the Indians. Many of our men had foolishly traded some of their weapons to the natives in exchange for buffalo robes or other furs, and Indian trinkets. They bitterly regretted their folly, when in addition to the warnings we had received, Dick told them of the imminent peril to which they were exposed. He sagely said that the natives always endeavored to trade their commodities for the white man's guns, as the first use they wished to put them to was to shoot these same "pale-faces" with their own weapons. Dick told us to be very cautious, to make no move without first consulting him. He felt positive that an attack would be made on us that night. He said that he would aid us in every possible way with his knowledge of the country and the Indians' mode of fighting.

Our men accordingly followed Dick's instructions explicitly, tethering the cattle close to the camp and grouping all the wagons as near together as was possible. About twilight, two naked and unarmed Indians were seen approaching. By signs they made us understand that they were hungry and wanted something to eat. Our men immediately consulted Dick and he advised them to give the savages all the food they wished and then secure them, so that they could not return to their friends. They were spies, Dick said, sent to see how many men we had, and how well-armed we were. After eating greedily, the two Indians lay down and pretended to be asleep. But we were satisfied that they were only playing "possum," and kept a close watch on them. A little later, as some of our men were coralling the cattle, according to Dick's instructions, several arrows came whizzing from out the grove of willows, in which the savages were concealed. One of these arrows passed through the brim of our man Williams' hat. This was getting rather close to danger, and our men lost no time in hastening back to camp, where they excitedly related their experiences, with the result that every able-bodied man immediately prepared for defense.

Dick said it would not be long now before the real struggle came, that the Indians were only waiting for darkness to shield them from our view. Of course there was intense excitement throughout the entire camp. We were compelled though, to keep perfectly silent, so that our savage foes might not discover our exact whereabouts. The women and children were huddled together, protected as much as they could be by the wagons, which were really no protection at all. It was little wonder that we were excited and nervous, for we all realized that a band of bloodthirsty Indians, many times our number, probably, was about to attack us. Of the result, we did not dare to guess. Naturally, we feared the worst. Visions of our husbands and friends slaughtered after enduring unspeakable tortures, and the women and children taken captive, filled our minds. Our situation was indeed dreadful. Even now, after the lapse of many years, the whole scene rises before me in all its ghastly details, and the awful horror of those few hours presses heavily upon my heart. Dick and his band were apparently friendly and sincere in their desire to aid us in repelling the savages, and upon their help and their loyalty we pinned our faith. If they should fail us, if they proved to be treacherous, as many of their race had been innumerable times before, we were lost indeed. Dick had told us, and we were obliged to believe him, that these natives hated him and his party as much as they hated us, and would stop at nothing to destroy them. He said that between them there was war to the knife, and no quarter.

Dick also said that in protecting us, he was only protecting himself and his men, for they would surely have been attacked, too. He and his people stood guard with ours, all ready, guns in hand, waiting for Dick to give the signal to fire.

It was a beautiful night, with no moon, but it was calm and starlit, the musical ripple of the creek as it flowed over its rocky bed was clearly audible to our ears. I remember thinking how strange and unreal it all seemed, and thoughts of distant friends and scenes recurred constantly to my mind. I wondered where they all were at that time, what they were doing and saying, and if they thought of us, far-away in the lonely and fearsome wilderness, surrounded by danger.

Soon after dark, while our guards stood motionless and watchful, they espied fifteen or twenty dusky figures creeping toward them. Nearer and nearer crept those crouching savages, our men still remaining motionless, until several arrows whizzed dangerously near our watchmen. Then, as the foes continued to advance steadily and stealthily, Dick gave the signal and our men fired. Instantly we heard screams and loud cries of pain from our assailants, mingled with the snapping and crackling of twigs as they fled in confusion. Dick told us afterwards that as they ran they cried out, "Run, boys, run! Very bad Americans after us!"

Dick and some of our men followed up the fleeing Indians for a short distance, but as it was now quite dark and the grove of willows afforded a fine screen for the skulking redskins, our men returned to camp. They fully expected that they would be attacked again before morning.

By this time there was a perfect panic in our midst. Women and children were screaming and wringing their hands and praying, declaring that we were all going to be killed. After the excitement had subsided somewhat, my sister and I went to bed and slept soundly until morning.

Most of the women stayed up all night, weeping and praying and imploring the men who were standing guard to be "careful," just as though the poor fellows were not using every possible precaution to save their lives, as well as ours. The women thought it was quite unfeeling for my sister and me to sleep through the night, when we all might have been murdered. I asked them why we should have remained up; told them that our presence could not help the men any, and that it only made it more difficult for them to protect us. I said to them that we needed all our strength and self-possession for the coming day, with the problems it might bring. But nothing I could say or do would convince them that we should not have stayed up to mingle our tears and prayers with theirs. They showed plainly that they considered us very cold and unsympathetic.

No other attempt was made to attack us during the night,

but you may be sure the entire camp felt wonderfully relieved when morning came. After it was fully light, with
faithful Dick and his party for guides, some of our men ex-
plored the place and the surroundings. The flight of the
savages was plainly marked by a trail of blood, proving that
the guns of our party and Dick's had done effective work.
Under a great tree, not far away, Dick's experienced eye de-
tected where nearly a hundred Indians had been encamped.
It is probable that more of them were close at hand.

We certainly felt grateful to Dick and his band, whose
presence and assistance had undoubtedly saved our lives. But
Dick was like all true heroes, modest and unassuming, de-
clining to accept most of the gifts we wished to shower upon
him from our scanty store. Naturally, we desired to leave
Rock Creek as soon as possible, and as we drove away from
the inhospitable place, after leaving warnings on many of
the trees for other emigrants, Dick and his company of kindly helpers rode off in the direction of the Missouri River,
leaving us, I must admit, with rather downcast hearts. The
last we ever saw of them was as they turned in their saddles,
their graceful little ponies standing quietly, to wave us a
friendly farewell. We fervently hoped that they would reach
their village in safety.

The two captive Indians we kept with us, according to
Dick's instructions, until we had gone several miles from the
vicinity of Rock Creek. Then we liberated them. They were
sullen and silent, and evidently much frightened. We
thought nothing could be gained, in any way, by detaining
them longer.

Later, we heard that the night following our experience
at Rock Creek, a large company of emigrants camping there
was attacked by Indians, probably the same band that had
attempted to annihilate us. There was a fierce, sharp struggle, and though the emigrants finally succeeded in beating
off the savages, two young men in the company received
wounds from poisoned arrows that afterwards caused their
death. I remember seeing one of these young men shortly

before he died. He was suffering greatly, and to make riding
in the rough wagon more comfortable and bearable for him,
his friends had arranged a sort of netted hammock, made of
rope, upon which a feather bed was placed, and the whole
slung between the sides of the wagon.

For some time now grass had been getting scarce and poor,
and our cattle were consequently growing weak and thin.
They were footsore and weary from their long, uninter-
rupted journey. We had passed through much alkali country
where both soil and water had been strongly impregnated
with this unwholesome substance, and two of our cows, three
of our oxen and our horse had already died from drinking
the alkali water. Often the ground would be white with
alkali, and as we had plenty of sour milk I frequently made
delicious biscuits and cakes with soda directly from Old
Mother Earth. In many places we saw magnificent cacti
growing, and they seemed to us like rare, tropical plants. So
delighted was I with them that I had one dug up very carefully, transplanting it with some of its native soil, intending
to carry it with me to our destination. However, after carrying it along for about a hundred miles, I threw it away.
Keeping it seemed too much like "carrying coals to New-
castle."

Most of us had hoped that after we left Fort Hall our
trials and privations would soon be ended, and that we would
speedily enter the Promised Land, otherwise known to us
as the Oregon Territory. But in this hope we were disappointed. Like Moses, we seemed destined never to reach it.
The hardest part of our long, tedious journey was yet to
come.

For some weeks past we had been traveling near the Snake
River, which is an unusually beautiful and interesting stream.
It was easy to understand why it had been named the Snake,
or the Serpent River, as the Indians called it, for its wind-
ings were devious and serpentine, and its waters often dark
and sullen. Frequently it wound its tortuous way through
rugged, towering walls black as night. Again, it would dance

and ripple along, the sun glinting on its surface, an object of tender loveliness, in strong contrast to its recent gloomy appearance. It was full of rapids and falls, some of the latter nearly two hundred feet in height. These scenes tended to increase the picturesque grandeur of the stream and impress the thoughtful traveler with its awesome, ever-changing character. To me this river was thoroughly typical of the country through which it flowed, mighty, fearsome, solitary, yet with its own wild beauty possessing attractions at once fascinating and wonderful.

It was on the banks of this interesting river that we first saw the salmon, those delicious fish so common here in Oregon that we do not properly appreciate them. We thought them the most toothsome fish we had ever tasted. We bought them fresh, dried and smoked from the friendly Indians we occasionally met, though our own fishermen partially supplied us with them. Immense sturgeon also abounded in the Snake, but only the Indians ate them in those days. The white people did not consider them fit for human consumption, as the sturgeon was supposed to be a "man-eater."

The country before and after reaching Fort Hall was extremely rough, making traveling slow and difficult for our weary animals. We traversed much lava formation and saw many evidences of volcanic action in huge, fantastic upheavals of stone and rock. These were always interesting to me, not only because of their curious forms, but also because they represented a condition of this old earth of ours vastly different from its present one, affording unlimited opportunities for speculation as to what it had once been.

After very hard traveling over a rough, hilly sage-brush country, interspersed with lava, we finally came to the Grande Ronde Valley—in Oregon Territory at last! You cannot imagine how beautiful this valley looked to us. It really seemed like a veritable bit of Paradise and I wanted to stay there forever. Many of the women were well satisfied with the country, but the men told us that we would all starve if we remained there, as it would be well-nigh impossible to get sufficient supplies to last us through the winter.

This splendid valley was like a big, round, green basin, surrounded with dark pine forests and wooded streams watering it abundantly. Our poor famished cattle enjoyed this lovely place quite as much as we did, for the grass there was fine and plentiful. Here we purchased new potatoes, the first we had seen since leaving Missouri, nearly six months before. From the Indian agent we bought fresh beef, which was also a luxury.

In our company was a poor Baptist minister with a large family of children, all clamoring for fresh vegetables and beef. But these things were so high-priced that the father felt he could not afford to purchase them. After considering the matter for a time, he bought a quantity of beef suet, with which he made gravy for his little ones, saying that from that they would get as much nourishment as from the meat.

After regretfully leaving this most delightful valley we went on our way over steep, rough, tree-clad hills until we came to the base of the dreaded Blue Mountains, where we found it rougher than ever. At last, after many efforts and disappointments, we succeeded in getting over these mountains, though it was slow, tedious work, as we were compelled to walk a goodly portion of the way, to save our weary and weak cattle. We passed through dark forests along the banks of numerous pretty streams and over grassy plateaus until at last we came into the Umatilla Valley, another magnificent section of country.

Here we again bought fresh beef and potatoes from an Indian agent. There were many Indians at Umatilla, nearly all of whom were dressed in white men's clothing, and all apparently friendly. The young squaws we thought especially attractive. They wore a quantity of gaudy finery and were usually mounted on fleet little Indian ponies, of which the women riders seemed almost a part, so adept were they in the management of their mounts. We had to tear ourselves away from Umatilla, also, for when we came to places where there was even a little civilization, the temptation to linger was strong. After leaving Umatilla our route wound through a very diversified region until we reached the John Day River, which we crossed without difficulty or delay. Oh! how ardently I would have liked to linger for a time in some of the fertile valleys and sylvan retreats through which we passed, and forget for a brief season, at least, the hardships and privations we had endured for so many months! But it was already September and we realized that we must hasten on to our destination, or perhaps be snowbound in the mountains, a fate that probably would have meant starvation for us all.

Long before reaching the Des Chutes country we came across many mute evidences of the jaded condition of the cattle in the trains preceding us. Feather beds, cook-stoves, chairs, tables, bedsteads, dishes, abandoned wagons and many, many other kinds of household furniture and utensils, all in good condition, strewed the ground for some distance. It was truly pathetic to see such awful waste in the wilderness, for we knew that all of these things were extremely valuable in a new country, such as the one to which we were journeying. Besides, it told us all too plainly what we might expect of the roads. I could not but think of the heartaches with which many of the women had parted from some treasured article of furniture, some piece, probably, that had been in their family for generations, and which had seemed too dear to leave behind in the safe old eastern home. Now, it was left to decay and rust among the lava rocks, the careless plaything of the elements, the coyotes and the rabbits.

When we finally reached the Des Chutes region we were obliged to do exactly what those before us had done, doubtless with no lighter hearts than ours. We cast aside every article that we could possibly spare. One wagon was shaved and whittled down as much as was consistent with strength and safety. All of our belongings were then put into this one, and the other perfectly good wagon left standing disconsolately beside the road. Oh, it was truly heart-breaking! But it had to be done. There was no use repining. Here, too, we parted with our cheery little sheet-iron cook stove, which had been a real joy and comfort to us all the way across the plains. Words cannot tell how I felt about leaving all these good things of ours, especially the stove, after we had carried them so far. I realized it would probably be a long time before I could get another such stove in the wild, new country to which we were going, that is, if we ever reached it. But there was no alternative. We simply could not carry these things, and it was both foolish and useless to grieve over them. But I can assure everybody that this ordeal required all the fortitude I could muster. Perhaps one thing that reconciled me was the thought that after all, we had much for which to be thankful. Then, too, most of us had already sacrificed so much in leaving our home that a little more did not matter materially.

Our cattle were now so weak they could hardly walk. Grass had been rather scarce recently, as many other trains had preceded us, and our animals had not been thoroughly rested since starting west. The poor creatures were literally worn out. They had been faithful and patient, but their labors were nearly done. I can see now how much wiser it would have been for us to have stopped every Sunday, just to have rested our poor, tired beasts.

Soon after crossing the Des Chutes River a cold rain began falling, and when we reached the Cascade Mountains a heavy snowstorm was raging. We therefore made camp near the base of the mountains for several days, resting our tired animals and waiting for the snow to cease. By this time it was quite deep. Many other parties of emigrants were camped near us, also resting and waiting for a favorable opportunity to cross over. Finally, after what seemed an eternity to us, the snow stopped falling and we bravely started on.

After much urging of our weary animals and much walking on our part, we succeeded after a long time, in getting about half-way over the mountains. Then we discovered, to our horror, that it was utterly impossible for us to proceed farther without help. Our cattle could not draw the wagon another yard. None of our companions could assist us, for they were in the same situation as ourselves. We were in despair. Winter was approaching. In fact, it was apparently already here. Our provisions were almost exhausted. We knew not which way to turn. We tried to walk over the mountains, leaving our cattle to their fate, but we found that impossible. One day I walked six miles, carrying my little girl, and at every step I sank deep in crusted snow. I remember that while I was walking I noticed numerous bushes of black huckleberries, and thought with relief that we would not really starve, at least not for awhile. The future certainly looked dark.

At last, after many days, the situation became so acute, with no immediate prospect of relief that some of the men, my husband among them, volunteered to attempt getting over the mountains to the other side in an effort to procure assistance. Oh, how we hated to see them go! With heavy hearts we watched them depart, fearing we would never see them again, for we knew not what dangers they might encounter in this venturesome and unknown journey.

However, after a day and a half of terrible anxiety and suspense on our part, we were overjoyed to see them returning with a number of other men and many fresh oxen. They had not gone far, they told us, when they met these kind people coming to our rescue. The settlers in the valley could tell from the signs that it was snowing in the mountains and they also knew that a great many emigrants were waiting there to cross over. They realized that if these new-comers were not aided soon, there would be much suffering, and perhaps death, among them. Never were men more gladly and gratefully welcomed than these good Samaritans. We felt, literally, like falling on their necks and weeping for joy. Among those who had come to help us was Mr. Allen, our companion of the plains, who had left us because we traveled on Sundays. He brought with him some of his sleek, fat oxen to draw the wagons that our jaded beasts could not pull. Another of the rescuing party was W. L. Adams, who later proved to be one of our best friends. With the assistance of this company of big-hearted men we were soon over the dreaded—and I might say "dreadful"—mountains. Then for the first time I felt that I was really in Oregon Territory.

The first stopping-place after crossing over the mountains was at Philip Foster's, where we obtained fresh beets, new potatoes, turnips and onions. After the men had arranged the camp for us, my husband and Mr. Adams went off to find a good place for the cattle to graze, and when they returned, my sister and I had supper ready—meat, vegetables and hot biscuits baked in a frying-pan over the open camp-fire. Mr. Adams was enthusiastic about the supper, stoutly declaring that it was the best meal he had ever eaten, and I have no hesitation in saying that we heartily agreed with him.

After resting at Foster's for two days, we went on to Oregon City, which we reached in about three days' travel, arriving there on the thirteenth day of September, 1851, almost six months from the time we had left Ohio. Mr. Adams insisted that we should go with him to his home in Yamhill County, and as we had no definite plans of our own, we were glad to accept his kind and friendly invitation.

While we remained in Oregon City for a few hours, so that Mr. Adams might get his mail and a few supplies, he left me with Mrs. Hood, wife of the merchant there. I was delighted to meet a pleasant, refined woman like her and felt that it was a good introduction to my new home. While we waited at Mrs. Hood's, her two pretty young daughters, one of whom was married, came in to see us, bringing us two delicious ripe peaches from their own garden. It seemed as though we had never seen such beautiful peaches or tasted any half so good. No gifts of gold could have surpassed them in our sight, for we were famishing for fresh fruit. I remember how surprised I was to see the two girls and their mother all so neatly dressed, both of the daughters wearing attractive black alpaca dresses. I had unconsciously expected to find the women in this new country clothed in primitive fashion, forgetting that most of them, like myself, were emigrants from old, highly-civilized communities and accustomed to the niceties of life.

While in Oregon City, which was merely a tiny village in the wilderness, we were repeatedly urged to remain and "take up claims." But this we declined to do, for we realized that we were strangers in a strange land, and for a time, at least, must submit ourselves to Mr. Adams' guiding hand. My sister had already left us, to go to another part of the Territory with some friends she had made on the westward journey, so my husband and I, with our little girl, were alone. Soon we left for Yamhill, which we reached on the morning of the second day after leaving Oregon City.

I had thought myself schooled to all sorts of changes and experiences, and flattered myself that I had considerable self-possession. But as the door of Mr. Adams' hospitable home closed behind me, I burst unexpectedly into tears. But they were tears of relief and joy, not of sorrow or regret. I realized that after six months of peril and privation, I was once more within the peaceful precincts of that most blessed of places—a home.

CHAPTER FIVE

VIEWING the country from the pleasant environs of Mr. Adams' home, my first impressions of Oregon Territory were really very agreeable. The Yamhill country was a beautiful agricultural district with fairly-well cultivated farms and rude farm houses situated about half a mile apart, in the neighborhood where I was. Most of the farms round about were located on what was known as "donation claims." These comprised three hundred and twenty acres of land for the smaller places and six hundred and forty acres for the larger ones.

Mr. Adams had proven himself a good friend to us, indeed, and we did not feel that we were wholly among strangers. In speaking of our family at home, we discovered that one of my sisters had married a distant relative of his with the same name as his own, so he called me "cousin," introducing me as such to his numerous friends and acquaintances.

He was a genial, kindly-hearted man of unusually fine intelligence. He was a brilliant conversationalist, with a refined, ready wit that always made him an entertaining and desirable companion. He was a graduate of Bethany College, in Virginia. He possessed a great appreciation of all that was best and finest in literature and the sciences. I remember how strange it seemed to me at first to find a man of Mr. Adams' mental attainments in this new, wild country. But later I realized how natural it was for a person of his intellectual type to seek a home in primitive, untried lands. Here was scope for his original talents and opportunities for growth and development such as he could not find in the older, more settled communities. As I became better acquainted with Mr. Adams, I understood why this great northwestern country had attracted him and others of his kind. In every respect he was a born pioneer of the highest type and tradition. The new, unsettled region appealed to his imagination because it was romantic and exciting. I came to realize that there were many like him in this far country to which I had so recently journeyed. They had vision, far more than I had. As I knew the people better, my respect for them increased. Mrs. Adams was an intelligent, sweet-tempered woman devoted to her family and her home, willing to let "William" manage everything, from the children to the farm. To know Mrs. Adams was literally to love her.

When it became known that I had at one time been a school teacher, I soon had plenty of opportunities to resume this work in my new home. Teachers were very scarce then. As my husband had not yet decided what we were going to do, or where we were going to be located, I finally yielded to the many importunities and commenced a private school in the family of a Mr. Norton, a farmer living near.

I had then been in the Territory about six weeks. Previous to beginning my school, I had met both Mr. and Mrs. Norton, and it was with some misgivings that I left my congenial companions, comfortable quarters and good meals at Mr. Adams'. I knew that conditions at Mr. Norton's would not be very homelike. But I tried to realize that I was now a pioneer, living under pioneer manners and conditions. Supper the first night at my new home consisted of hot biscuits, very large and coarse, milk, "jerked" beef, the latter prepared on the place, naturally. It was put on the table in large chunks, and each person was supposed to cut off as much of it as he desired. The table was covered with an old colored oil-cloth and tin cups were provided for the milk. There was no butter and it was several days before Mrs. Norton found it convenient to churn some. However, the Nortons were generous providers in their primitive way, but shiftless and extremely poor managers.

When the first Saturday came round, I prepared to do some of my family laundry work. My husband, who had just returned from a fruitless prospecting tour, carried water from the "branch," as the Nortons called the creek, filled the washboiler and placed it over the open fire for me. Mrs.

Norton was a deeply interested spectator of these proceedings, and finally she remarked, rather sadly, "The Yankee men are so good to their wives, they help 'em so much!"

After that, I frequently noticed Mr. Norton's way of "helping" his wife. He would stroll in leisurely, after his work or his lounging was over, look around critically, peer into the water bucket, and would then call out loudly, in a tone that brooked no delay, "Mary Jane, I want some water! This bucket's empty!"

And poor Mary Jane, weary and uncomplaining, would stop her dinner getting or put down her fretful baby and run with alarcity to the spring to "fetch" water for her lord and master. Yet her husband was not unkind to her. It was just his way.

Mr. Norton was an illiterate man and therefore much impressed by the "larnin' of the Yankee school-ma'am," as he called me. My school room adjoined the family kitchen, with a sort of Dutch door, separated in the middle, between the two rooms. Nearly every day Mr. Norton would come and lean his big, brawny arms over the lower part of this door, listening in rapt attention to the regular school routine. Often I would see his keen blue eyes gleam with pride and pleasure at one of his children's recitations. Frequently he would slap his plump sides and exclaim in his hearty, genuine way, "Wal, ye do knaow a heap, school-ma'am. I'd give a thousand dollars if I knowed jest half as much!" Although the Nortons lived in most primitive fashion, having no comforts whatever in their home, and in fact hardly having the bare necessities of life at times, they were by no means poor people.

They owned one hundred and sixty acres of fine farming land and many cattle and horses. Mr. Norton was often heard to say that he had a hundred horses, each one worth a hundred dollars. He was a Kentuckian, and occasionally he would drawl out, in his soft southern accent, "Genl'men, I doesn't wuk with a pick or a shovel, I wuks on hossback!"

He had once been a member of an expedition that had

pursued and engaged in battle with the Indians in another part of the Territory. He was extremely fond of relating his experiences and adventures while with this party. His children listened with absorbed interest and eagerness to their father's highly-colored accounts of this incident, of which he was always the Don Quixote. The first time I heard this story of his, I nearly exploded with suppressed laughter, not at the tale itself, but at some of Mr. Norton's quaint expressions.

In describing the attack of his party upon a supposedly small band of Indians and discovering too late that the savages had tricked the whites and had a great many warriors in concealment, he said, "Arter we attackted 'em, we discivered that there was more than a thaousand Injins in ambier." But anyway, the clever white men completely vanquished their savage foes, and that was the main point to be considered.

At Christmas time Mrs. Norton gave a large party, inviting people from many miles around. Like most western women of that day, she was a poor cook, as she herself realized. Accordingly, it fell to my happy lot to make all the dainties for this occasion. When Mrs. Norton asked me to assist her with the cooking for this party, she added, as though apologizing for the request, "You Yankee women are such good cooks!" It was a genuine pleasure to do anything for this good-hearted family. They were all appreciative and appeared to thoroughly enjoy my cooking. I can hardly describe how much I enjoyed getting ready for this big party. While I was beating eggs, mixing cakes and making pies and preserves, I could almost imagine myself back in dear old Ohio, preparing for a big, old-fashioned dinner to which all the relatives were coming. It did not seem in the least like Christmas to me, for there was no snow on the ground and the evergreen trees kept all their foliage, instead of showing bare branches, as our eastern maples, elms and nut trees did.

The party was a huge success. People came from far and

near. Dancing began at seven in the evening and continued until nearly seven the following morning. Then the farmers had to go home to milk their cows, even if it was Christmas Day. The school room, which was used as the ballroom, was lighted with homemade tallow candles or "dips," and the rustic fiddler that sawed away on his squeaky old violin sent forth such entrancing strains as "Pop Goes the Weasel," "The Arkansas Traveler," "The Girl I Left Behind Me," and "Old Rosin the Beau." The freckled-faced youth that officiated as "caller" fairly bawled himself hoarse in a frantic effort to be heard above the dancers' shuffling feet and merry voices.

In the low-ceilinged "front room" some of the older people sat around the spacious, blazing fireplace, telling marvelous tales of pioneer experiences, of hair-breadth "escapes from Injins" and "varmints," and varied fortunes and misfortunes, each one striving to outdo the other in strange and thrilling stories. The supper table fairly groaned under its load of good things. There were speeches, wise and otherwise, by the prominent men gathered there from many different states. Some of the men present that evening afterwards received the highest political gifts in the power of their community to bestow. Mr. Norton had opened a barrel of whiskey for this special occasion. Well-to-do farmers who enjoyed intoxicants usually bought their liquor by the barrel in those days. Of course everybody was privileged to help himself to the "fire water" whenever he felt so inclined. Nevertheless, despite this opportunity for over-indulgence, I can truthfully say that not one intoxicated person was seen there that night. I wonder if that could be said of so large a company gathered together under similar circumstances nowadays?

After teaching at Nortons for four months, I went to another district, where I had a much larger school, nine of the pupils in the former place coming to me in the new location. This time I was to live at the home of Judge Eldon, who had a very large family, not all, however, of school age.

The Eldons were delightful, intellectual people, but extremely poor housekeepers. They seemed utterly indifferent as to what they ate or to how their meals were prepared. They considered eating a necessary evil, a waste of precious time that might be more pleasantly and profitably employed. Of course, this was not a very satisfactory condition of affairs for me, with my strait-laced eastern ideas concerning housekeeping in general.

In this careless household the dishes were always wiped with the same dirty-looking rag with which they had been washed, after it had been wrung as dry as possible. Occasionally, I dried the dishes for the girls and always insisted upon getting a clean white cloth for that purpose, much to the amusement of the entire family, who laughingly declared that "the Yankee women are so particular!"

Every meal I would find half a teaspoonful, or more, of dishwater in my cup. I invariably wiped it out with a corner of my white apron—we all wore aprons in those days—and though my action was plainly visible, as I intended it should be, as I took no pains to conceal it, no apologies or improvements were ever made.

The Eldons had a fine large farm, with many cows, but for the first six weeks of my stay there we had neither milk or butter, simply because they were too indifferent and indolent to attend to the matter. When we finally began having butter, I enjoyed it immensely, until one day when I happened to pass through the kitchen where Mary, one of the girls, was working it with her hands. The sight of the soft, oily substance running through her red fingers sickened me so that I could not taste it again.

The biscuits at the Judge's were unique in their way, and if I dared to perpetrate a pun, I might say in their "weigh" as well. They were made of flour, salt and water mixed into a hard, stiff dough, and cut into rounds about four inches in diameter and three inches thick. Then they were baked in the oven for two hours. Frequently, in fact usually, they were burned black on both top and bottom. We had them for breakfast, dinner and supper, and I never heard one of the family make any complaint concerning them except that once the Judge said mildly to his daughter, as he patiently sawed away on a cold, burnt biscuit, "Jane, I wish you would make your biscuits a little smaller. I'd like to get a hot one occasionally!"

Finally a longing for some of my own good biscuits grew upon me. One evening I plucked up courage and said to Jane, as she was preparing for supper, "Jane, I think I can beat you making biscuits!" Jane opened her blue eyes wide in astonishment, but she only replied, indifferently, "Can you?"

"Let me make some for supper tonight," I coaxed. "You have quantities of wonderful sour cream there!"

"All right," she laughed. "If you want to make them, you can."

I went to my task delightedly. I had great success with the biscuits, dainty little affairs that baked a beautiful golden-brown in ten minutes. Rather curious to know the family's opinion of them as contrasted with their own kind, I mentally counted the number that each one ate. I was delighted to perceive that the Judge took nine, while Jim, the eldest son, ate ten with evident satisfaction.

I thought that the biscuits were delicious, and apparently the others thought the same, but not one word was said about them by any member of the family, except by Mrs. Eldon, who remarked as she reached for a fifth one, "They're nice, ain't they?"

However, that was my first and last experience in making biscuits at Judge Eldon's, for they never asked me to make any more, and naturally, I could not proffer my services again. The undoubted inference was that they preferred their biscuits to mine.

A few weeks later when they were expecting some special guests for tea, they came to me in great embarrassment, asking if I would make some cake for the occasion. Of course I was delighted to do so, and used one of my tried old re-cipes from home, baking the cakes in little patty-pans I had brought from Ohio. The reception accorded the cakes was by no means as chilling as that given the biscuits. Everybody actually raved over them, not only during the meal, but afterwards as well. They were the favorite topic of conversation in the household for days while the cookies were treasured for weeks, being brought out only occasionally as a great "treat."

Under the bed in my room, which had cracks in the walls so wide that I could almost put my fingers through them, there was a heterogeneous mass of old boots, shoes and discarded clothing from the different members of the family. These had evidently been accumulating for several years. This accumulation extended from the floor to the straw mattress above, and the odor arising from this mouldy, dirty and decaying rubbish was anything but agreeable or healthful.

One day when I was cleaning the room, I remarked to Annie, one of the daughters, that if she would tell me where to put the things I would take them out from under the bed. Saying that she would ask her mother, she disappeared, returning in a few minutes, however, with the cheering intelligence that "Maw said not to bother, that they were all right there."

Although Judge Eldon was a well-educated man who stood high in his community and had been honored with many political offices, he had some peculiar forms of expression that seemed amusing to me. He had probably acquired these ungrammatical phrases through living among illiterate people for several years in his youth.

The Eldons had neither corn nor potatoes in their garden because their rail fences were not kept in sufficiently good order to exclude the cattle. Frequently I have seen the Judge look up from a book in which he had for some time been absorbed, to see a solitary ox grazing peacefully among the scanty vegetables, and he would cry hurriedly, "Run, children, and drive that oxen out of the garden!"

My school house was half a mile from the Eldon home, and during February of that year, 1852, the weather was so mild that I wore thin slippers to school the entire month, without even once getting my feet damp. In March, however, heavy snow covered the ground, lingering for some time. This gave me an opportunity to wear the high calfskin boots that my husband had made for me before we left Ohio, thinking that we might be obliged to go through regions infested with snakes. But I never had the boots on all the way across the plains, though they came in handy enough now. In February the wild strawberries were in bloom, and in June these delicious berries were so plentiful everywhere that the paths of the wagon wheels, in the more unfrequented parts of the country, were marked by a trail of vivid, crushed red fruit.

When I first went to Judge Eldon's, I was quite plump, and my dresses would hardly "meet around me," but owing to their poor and unwholesome food, and their method of preparation, at the end of three months, my clothes lapped over a full finger's length. I think I would have faded away almost entirely if I had not gone to Mr. Adams' home every Friday night to remain until the following Monday morning. Mrs. Adams was a fine cook and a generous provider. She was a native of the grand old state of Maine, where her early girlhood had been spent. Sometimes Judge Eldon, belated on his way home, would stop for a meal at Mr. Adams, and after disposing of a liberal allowance of good things, he would shake his head and say with affected seriousness, "Ah, Brother William, you'll die of dyspepsia yet!" And "Brother William" would retort good-naturedly, "I'd rather die of dyspepsia than starvation, as you'll do!"

It was during these week-end visits at Mr. Adams that I first heard his celebrated melodrama, entitled "Brakespeare, a Political Satire." He read it to me week by week as he wrote it and it certainly was remarkably clever and interesting. If I remember correctly, it was first published in the *Weekly Oregonian,* which was then owned and edited by T. J. Dryer. It created quite a sensation as it satirized a number of men prominent in Oregon Territorial politics.

Later, it was published in book form and it has been said that it was the first original book to be written and published in the Territory. The Whigs, now the Republicans, were delighted with this satire and it had a wide circulation for those days. A few years later, Mr. Adams founded and edited a weekly newspaper called the *Argus*, which his political opponents were pleased to refer to as the "Airgoose."

In religion Mr. Adams was a Campbellite, which sect had quite a wide following in the Territory, and when the regular minister was absent, which was frequently the case, Mr. Adams preached to the congregation. Because of this, he was sometimes designated as "Parson Billy."

I remember the exact appearance of his melodrama as it was first published. It was illustrated with crude wood-cuts, the first representing the outside of a rough country grocery store. A man was mounted on the top of a huge barrel piled high with bacon, while he thus addressed the crowd standing near: "Attention, tillicums, whilst I, standing on a more firmer foundation, proceed to drop a few impertinent remarks without any diabolical flourish or logical circumlocution," etc., etc.

Attending my school were four or five young men, some of them almost as old as myself, and as many grown girls. Therefore it was not surprising that the sly little god, Cupid, found a way to enter. Before the school had been closed for a week, a wedding occurred between two of my former pupils. As the circumstances connected with it were rather unusual, you may be interested in hearing about them. These two young people were first cousins, the boy just twenty years old, the girl only seventeen. Their attachment to each other had long been known to their respective families, and because of their relationship and their youth, bitterly opposed.

One morning, however, the boy, a fine, manly young fellow, walked into the presence of his sweetheart's father, saying simply, "Uncle Richard, Lucy and I are going to be married next Sunday!" The father held up his hands in horror and began to pour forth a violent torrent of objections. But the boy cut him short.

"Uncle Richard," he repeated firmly, "we are going to get married, and nothing that you can say or do will prevent it. If you are willing, we will be married here, at Lucy's home. If not, we'll run away!" The father reflected briefly. He was sensible enough to perceive that further remonstrance was useless. So he did what most parents would do under similar circumstances—he gave a reluctant consent.

The simple ceremony occurred the following Sunday morning, immediately after church and just before dinner. After the meal, not a particularly joyous one, the youthful groom rode his horse around to the front door, and the little bride, with all her trousseau in a "carpet bag," climbed up behind him. Thus a future governor of Oregon and his pretty girl-wife rode off to the new life that was to be theirs.

CHAPTER SIX

ALTHOUGH I had now been absent from civilization—otherwise Ohio—for more than a year, I was still considered an authority on matters of dress and fashion. I was consulted and acted as adviser whenever a new cloak or gown was made, or even contemplated. I trimmed hats, literally, for the entire neighborhood, and I knew less than nothing about millinery.

Before leaving Ohio I had realized that it might be difficult for me to find suitable or satisfactory clothes in the new Oregon Territory, so I had laid in a fairly-good supply, especially of dresses, sufficient to last me for two or three years. I was glad that I had done this, as I found the selection, particularly in women's clothes, very meager indeed. I had a number of silk dresses, as that material was always good and wore well. These silk dresses "packed" well, requiring small space. My brown taffeta wedding gown was still presentable, despite the fact that the bodice was becoming a little snug, as my former slender figure was beginning to assume more matronly proportions. I recall our two well-worn leather trunks, thickly studde with brass-headed nails in intricate designs, that held my "wardrobe." These trunks were never once opened on the plains, though I had occasion to open them frequently enough after I reached my new home.

I wonder now what ever became of those old trunks! I have not thought of them before for years. I suppose they appeared to outlive their usefulness and were given away to someone that needed them more than we. Well, they would be antiques now, and would be found in some museum, probably. The girls of the Eldon family adored my brown taffeta, especially the lovely white embroidered undersleeves that accompanied it. Speaking of undersleeves reminds me of some I used to see when I was a child of eight years, as a pupil in "the little red schoolhouse" in New York state. I sat between two grown girls whose balloon-like dress sleeves with their feather under-sleeves, almost hid from sight the small figure seated between them.

I distinctly recall that we were studying "geography of the heavens," as simple astronomy was called then. I remember how I loved this study and I recollect the exact words found in my text-book regarding Orion, my favorite constellation. These words were: "This constellation is too-splendidly-beautiful to be described." All my life I have loved Orion, with its "belt of gold." I am sure I used to give my gentle mother many moments of uneasiness when I insisted upon remaining outdoors after dark to trace the constellations.

All my life, too, I have loved the heavens, with their calm, mysterious splendor and their unfathomed, starry depths.

I have indeed "lifted up mine eyes" to them, finding hope and consolation in their friendly serenity and far-off glory.

But getting back to clothes and styles. The entire Eldon family wore my clothes—theirs always needed mending—and they were only prevented from wearing my shoes because they were too small.

All kinds of provisions, dress goods, and in fact, all other things, were naturally much higher-priced here than in the east. This was largely owing to the expense and difficulty of getting goods into this new country. I remember a little circumstance that brought vividly to my observation the difference in prices here and at home. One day I went with some members of the family to the village of Lafayette, ten miles away. I had promised the children that I would bring them some candy, so I told the clerk that waited on me at the store to give me ten cents' worth. In Ohio this would have been ten sticks. The clerk looked at me a little curiously and to my surprise wrapped up only *one* stick. I glanced at it and remarked, "I wanted *ten* cents' worth!" He looked at me again, smiled, hesitated and then asked, "You are from the east, ain't you? Here we sell one stick of candy for ten cents!" "Oh," I ejaculated, a light breaking in upon me, "give me a dollars' worth, then!"

According to the Oregon Donation law in force at that time, every citizen—women were not considered "citizens" then—of the United States over eighteen years of age and married, was entitled to "take up" six hundred and forty acres of land, one-half of which was to be his wife's, in her own right. If single, a man could take but three hundred and twenty acres. This condition of affairs naturally encouraged every bachelor in the Territory speedily to become a benedict. As a result, many matrimonial abuses developed. Young women of suitable age for marriage were few in the Territory. Thus girls of tender age were sacrificed to greed.

I personally knew of one case where a child of four years was married to a mature man, the "husband" leaving for the mines immediately after the ceremony. Another case that came under my observation was that of a girl of eleven years, who was married to a man of twenty-eight. Several months after this marriage some of my friends spent the afternoon with the little wife, who was a relative of theirs. She helped her husband prepare the supper for their guests, but after the meal was finished she disappeared. Finally she was found in the back yard, having a glorious time with a neighbor's little girl, "teetering" on a board thrown over a log. The husband came back into the house, cleared the table and washed the dishes, remarking as he did so, "Lizzie's young yet!" I'd say that she was!

One Sunday at church my attention was called to a pretty, delicate looking girl, who also had been married at eleven years of age. She held a baby of four or five months in her arms and another child of about two years stood by her side. These immature marriages, these crimes against nature, as they seemed to me, used to make my old-fashioned "Yankee" blood fairly boil with righteous wrath.

Some of the more pleasant recollections of my stay in Yamhill are connected with the family of Dr. John McBride, in whose hospitable home I spent many delightful days. At the time of my acquaintance with the McBrides, they had twelve children. No "race suicide" there. Not all of these children were of school age, however. Some were grown, and others were mere babies. I believe that four more children were born to the McBrides later.

Both the doctor and his wife, Mahala, which I always thought a wonderfully sweet name, were pioneers of 1846. The doctor was a prominent man in his neighborhood, as well as in the Territory at large. He was the first state school superintendent in this entire region, having been elected to that office at the Territorial Legislature held in Oregon City in July, 1846. Later, he was honored with many other offices of trust and distinction. He was a Tennesseean by birth, but had been educated mainly in Missouri. His sister, Mrs. Caleb Wood, who had crossed the plain with her brother and his family, lived near and their association at that time was very intimate and beautiful. I think the entire McBride family was as talented and interesting as any I ever knew. Mrs. McBride was quite an unusual woman, calm, dignified, sweet-tempered and most charitable in word and deed. The care of her large family rested lightly upon her, and so exemplary were they all that I doubt if they ever gave their parents a moment of uneasiness. The McBrides were really a remarkable family. Many of them distinguished themselves later in manifold worthy ways, being honored with positions of importance in various fields.

For some time now my husband had been "prospecting" in the country, looking for the elusive gold mine that he always hoped to find. In July, 1852, he came for me and our little girl and we went down to the Umpqua Valley, where he had located a claim of three hundred and twenty acres, at a place called "Camas Swale."

I was indeed sorry to leave the good, kind friends I had found in Yamhill, but our paths were destined to sever, nevermore to meet. They were all fine, hospitable people, and I shall never forget their innumerable kindnesses to me, an utter stranger in their midst. The word "Swale" means a low, usually marshy or swampy place, or a sort of depressed valley, if I may so describe it. In this case, it was a big, beautiful green meadow. Here abounded the camas, a bulbous plant that was to the Indians in early days what wheat is to the white people now. In taste, the camas somewhat resembles an ordinary potato. The Indians cooked it, most often baking it in hot ashes, and then ground it in their stone mortars, which we call their "grist mills." Then it was shaped into loaves or flat cakes mixed with water, baked in hot ashes or on heated stones, and it was really quite palatable and very nourishing. The plant bears a pretty blue flower in springtime. I have frequently heard this called the "wild onion," though it is nothing like an onion either in appearance or taste. The Indians used to come in great numbers to Camas Swale, camping there for weeks, digging and drying the camas for winter use.

We used to see many native dances and games while the Indians were encamped near us, but I never was much interested in them. People today would enjoy them immensely, I suppose, as they were very picturesque. I had too wholesome a fear of the natives and their possible treachery to find enjoyment in anything they did. Since those early days I have often regretted that I did not take more interest in the Indians—in their customs, manners and legends. In this way I would have had a clearer, better understanding of these unusual people.

After we moved to Camas Swale, while our log cabin was being built of logs hewed by hand from the virgin forest, we lived for about two months in a tent.

There were many rattlesnakes in that vicinity. I could rarely go to the spring, a few rods distant, without seeing at least one, and frequently I saw several of these venomous creatures. I kept a sharp lookout on my little girl to see that she did not stray far from my side. One day I lost her, and it seemed as though I would never find her again. I hunted everywhere, called her by name loudly and repeatedly, but only the mocking echoes of my own voice answered me. A band of Indians had passed our way a few days before, and I was tormented with the thought that they had returned and kidnaped the pretty little white child. This fear made me almost frantic. I was entirely alone that day, as my husband had gone up the valley on business. After I had looked in every conceivable place where I imagined she might possibly be, I was returning disconsolately and quite beside myself to the tent. As I was passing a great tree whose drooping branches almost touched the ground, I caught a glimpse of her pink dress through the leaves.

Overjoyed, I rushed to the spot, and parting the heavy branches, I looked down upon my daughter's smiling, roguish face.

"Oh, my darling," I cried rapturously, as I caught her to my breast, "Mother thought she had lost her baby, and she was so frightened."

"Was 'oo f'ightened, modder," she lisped. "Baby was p'ayin' house in dis p'itty t'ee."

While we were living in the tent, I had what seemed to me quite a thrilling experience. No matter how long I live, I shall not forget that little incident. It is not one I would ever wish to repeat, even though it might again end happily. One extremely warm afternoon I put my little girl to bed for her usual nap. As was my custom, I lay down beside her for a few moments. The child soon fell asleep, and as I was about to rise from the bed I saw a sight that seemed to paralyze every nerve and muscle in my body. In the tent, close by the head of the bed stood a large chest that we had brought from Ohio, and which we then used as a table. A foot or so away from this chest, and parallel with it, was an old-fashioned, brass-studded leather trunk, which we had also brought across the plains. This trunk was not as high as the chest by perhaps eighteen inches. As I glanced up, preparatory to rising, the head of a large rattlesnake appeared between the chest and the trunk, scarce a hand's breadth from the bed. I could have touched the creature from where I lay. I seemed absolutely petrified when my astonished eyes first rested on this hideous thing. But it was for a very brief period that I remained in that condition. With startling reality I understood that something had to be done, and done quickly, too, if my life and my child's were to be saved.

There was no one near to help me. My husband was working at our cabin a quarter of a mile away, and could not have reached me in time to save us, even if he had heard my cries for assistance. It was "up" to me to save the situation. I simply had to work out my own salvation. But I did not know what to do. All sorts of ideas and schemes rushed through my bewildered brain in a moment, but the main thought underlying it all was that I must somehow get off the bed speedily and find the axe. With this thought uppermost, I began working my way quietly but very rapidly to the foot of the bed, the horrid creature watching me constantly with its bright, beady eyes, its tongue darting angrily back and forth as it hissed its displeasure. It seemed like an eternity to me until I succeeded in getting off the bed. Then I ran like mad to the outside of the tent where the axe lay beside the woodpile. Seizing it, I darted back into the tent.

On the outer side of the low trunk, I could still see some of the snake's tail, and I knew that it could not spring until its body was entirely out in the open space between the chest and the trunk. Now, with the friendly axe held cautiously in my hand, I approached the trunk on the side toward me. Suddenly, the creature put its head down on the ground, drawing the tail out of sight, probably preparing to coil and spring. Instantly, then, I was up on the trunk, axe in hand, and then, nerved to desperation, I brought the heavy end of the axe down on the snake's head, grinding, grinding, grinding slowly and fiercely, literally working for life itself.

I continued to grind heavily upon the reptile's head for several minutes, not daring to stop for fear it might not yet be dead. I knew all too well that a wounded and maddened rattlesnake was far more to be feared than an unharmed one. Finally, after what seemed an interminable length of time to me, I took courage and cautiously lifted up the axe. To my inexpressible joy and relief, I found that the creature was motionless. No need for me to say that I felt like shouting, and then suddenly I grew very faint. I think almost anyone would have felt the same way under similar circumstances. But I do not believe that I uttered a sound. I was too overcome for that. But though I had succeeded in destroying the enemy that would have taken our lives, I was not satisfied to have the horrible thing in the tent with me and my child. But how was I to get it out of the tent?

I finally evolved a plan that I thought would succeed. I went outside, found a long stick, returned to the tent and gradually drew the horrid creature out into the air. Then, in some way, I never knew just how, I managed to transfer it to a wide board that I stood up against a post where I could watch it from inside the tent to see if the snake showed any signs of returning life.

It had not hung there more than an hour when two horse-men rode up. They exclaimed in surprise when, in answer to their questions, I told them where and how I had killed the rattler. Dismounting immediately, they counted the rattles, finding seven and a button. However, I am happy to say that this was my first and last encounter with a rattlesnake. I was well satisfied to have it so.

It happened that one day soon after we had moved into our new house, otherwise our little log cabin, I had just finished baking some pies when two hungry men came along. As soon as their eyes fell upon these tempting golden-brown morsels, they wanted to buy them from me. I had no reason for refusing to sell them, especially as the men were hungry and willing to pay for them. We had already given scores of meals to the hungry men that were continually passing back and forth from the mines to the settlements. These people always offered to pay for their food, for the early settlers were more than generous, but according to the old-fashioned code of hospitality then in vogue, we had always declined to accept their money. However, it was beginning to be rather a serious matter.

I was known far and wide as a good cook, and men made it a point to reach our place, sometimes walking four or five miles after dark, to stay there for the night. We had a huge fireplace with plenty of big logs to burn. The cabin was clean, cheerful and fairly comfortable. Provisions were expensive, and we really could not afford to feed these hungry people for nothing. They were all complete strangers to us and we rarely saw them again after we had fed them of our best. The sudden sale of the two fresh pies gave me an idea. After thinking the matter over seriously, I concluded that we were under no obligations whatever to cook and work for the hungry horde that was continually passing our door. If we were obliged to provide for them, as it seemed we were, and I was expected to do all the work, I might as well have pay for it. I lost no time in putting my new plan to work. I painted a primitive sign on a shingle with these words, "Pies for Sale." I was just nailing this against the side of the cabin when a good Samaritan came along and made a better sign for me, fixing it in place properly.

Before the sign had been there half an hour, two travelers rode up. Perceiving the sign, they alighted immediately from their horses and purchased two pies. They seemed delighted at the opportunity to buy good home-made pies and complimented them highly. One of these men was Addison C. Gibbs, afterwards governor of Oregon. He was returning from a trip to Scottsburg, on the Umpqua River, where he was interested in a new townsite. I charged fifty cents apiece for custard, dried apple and peach pies, and a dollar each for those made of my fine home-made mincemeat. That first memorable afternoon I took in five dollars. The first week my proceeds were fifty dollars. I could have sold twice as many as I did if I could have found time to make them. In two months I took in three hundred dollars for pies and little cakes, served with a glass of fresh milk. I received fully as much more for meals. Then I fell ill from overwork and was obliged to take down the sign.

Still men flocked to our place. Grass was fine around there

and traders and miners brought their mules to graze and recuperate in the lush meadows. We were young people, anxious to get on in the world, and we felt that we could not afford to stop the immensely profitable business of selling cakes and pies and serving meals to hungry travelers. But I was unable to do the work. Then my husband tried to take my place. He made pies under my directions, following them explicitly and was really very successful. We had many a hearty laugh over this unique experience, such as many early pioneers probably had. I was in bed for two weeks and for another week sat helplessly by while Freeman worked. He would not allow me to lift even a plate. At the end of three or four weeks I was physically able to resume my work, though by this time it had grown to be somewhat monotonous and irksome. There was no longer any joy in it for me, it had lost all its thrill. The novelty of earning money in that way had worn off.

A little later, when the season was more advanced, my husband bought a quantity of wheat from some farmers, paying them ten dollars a sack for it. He took it to the mill and had it ground and afterwards sold it so that he made a profit of five hundred dollars on the transaction.

The winter of 1852-1853 was unusually cold and severe. Deep snow covered the ground in many places and cattle and horses were starving everywhere. Freeman took two hundred pounds of flour to the mines near Jacksonville and sold it there for two hundred dollars. The miners and few settlers in that locality were glad to get it at any price. The heavy snow made travel to the mines very slow and difficult and often times dangerous. The imprisoned miners looked with joy upon anyone that brought in any sort of provisions. A man really took a chance on his life in attempting to get into that region at that time. He was liable to be overtaken by snow and perish through losing his way. While my husband was absent on this trip to the mines, I also sold a quantity of flour, at the rate of thirty dollars for a fifty-pound sack.

But just as matters seemed so prosperous with us, though

we were both working very hard and earning all we made, my little girl fell ill and I was obliged to devote most of my time to her. The deaf young nursemaid I had employed for the child had to leave me, as her mother died suddenly, leaving an infant daughter to the older sister's care. Our hired man also became sick and had to be nursed, so we had our hands more than filled with our own private affairs for a time.

We had now been at Camas Swale six months and were making money very fast. But my husband thought we might do much better at a place called Canyonville, twenty miles from Rose's place, or as it is called now, Roseburg. We accordingly sold our claim at Camas Swale. There were plenty of men glad to take it off our hands at a good price, and my husband bought another claim of three hundred and twenty acres at Canyonville.

Presently, my husband went into partnership with a man who owned a long log hotel. It was very prosperous. In seven months they had each cleared twenty-five hundred dollars. I did not have much work to do at Canyonville. In fact, I took life very easy indeed. I think I was pretty well exhausted by my former strenuous experiences to which I had never before been accustomed. Both Freeman and I felt that we had done very well at Canyonville. Twenty-five hundred dollars was quite a tidy bit of money in those days! We had acquired this in a comparatively short time, too.

We kept supplies of men's rough, common clothing and many other articles that miners, trappers and packers would naturally require. We bought all our goods direct from peddlers who came to the place. There was no other way for us to procure them. We paid high prices for everything, of course, but we sold them for a still higher price, making a good profit. One day I bought three hundred dollars' worth of goods, paying for them in gold dust, which was a common form of currency then, though steps had been taken by the Territory to prevent it being kept in circulation because of its bulkiness and the loss from frequent divisions.

My husband was gone much of the time while we lived at Canyonville, either to the mines, for he was always hoping that he would "strike it rich," or on some political mission. He had very soon become interested in politics, with which the whole Territory was rife. He was a born orator, a logical and interesting speaker, and his services were always in demand. Public speaking was no new business to him.

While we remained at Canyonville we had many unusual and extremely interesting experiences. We met a number of persons that afterwards became well-known characters locally. One picturesque figure that I remember well was "Captain Jane," rather a pretty young woman about thirty years of age. Invariably, she was dressed in men's clothing, which was uncommon and made her a conspicuous figure in those early days. She was a frequent visitor on her trips back and forth to the mines from California. She had her own pack-train of mules and made a good living by carrying supplies to the miners. Though she lived in the midst of rough characters, apparently consorting freely with them, and to all appearances leading the life of an ordinary packer, she never permitted any familiarities from those she met. The men always spoke of her in a respectful manner. I understood at the time that she had been left a penniless widow with several small children and had adopted this work because it paid well.

While in Canyonville I had another little experience that was rather unusual, one that might not have ended as happily as it did. One balmy evening my husband and I were sitting on the big, rustic front porch discussing our plans for the future. Suddenly, I was startled to hear a sound like a baby crying lustily in the woods on the hill above. I exclaimed to my husband about it, wondering if it could be possible that a child was lost and wandering out there in the forest. But he dismissed the subject lightly, saying that it was probably the voice of some bird with which we were unfamiliar. Later in the evening I again heard that strange, wild cry, and several times during the night I was awakened by it, now sounding much nearer. It gave me an indescribable sensation of fear, it was so uncanny, so unusual, so full of a certain dread significance.

In the morning my husband spoke of it, telling me that the cry we had heard the night before was that of a panther or cougar, as they are sometimes called. He said we must watch our little girl and see that she did not stray far from the house, as panthers had been known to carry off small children. After that, I heard no more of the creature and naturally concluded that it had gone to some other locality, more remote from the haunts of men where small game, like young fawns, were more plentiful.

A few weeks after this, my husband went out hunting, returning a few hours later with a fine, big deer. He dressed it and hung it up in a little shack adjoining the house where we kept our meat and some other perishable things. There was an opening in the shack about the size of a small window to provide fresh air and ventilation. Ordinarily, this opening was covered with a cloth, but at the time of which I speak there happened to be nothing over it. Just about dusk that evening it occurred to me that there was something in the shack that I wanted, so I went around the house to get it. As I unlatched the rude door, I heard a peculiar sound, but thought nothing of it. Pushing open the door, I was about to enter when, to my horror, I perceived a long, tawny animal standing up on its hind legs and eating greedily away at our deer. As the creature caught sight of me, it paused in its stolen repast, dropped to the ground like a flash and with a hideous snarl that showed its cruel white teeth, it sprang at me. With a terrified scream I fell to the ground, and the panther, for such it was, carried by its momentum a little distance beyond me, jumped to its feet and sped away into the dusk. Probably it was as much frightened as I, for of course it had never before seen a woman. I suppose, that is, if a panther thinks at all, it thought of me as some strange new sort of animal which would naturally be an enemy.

About this time fresh troubles arose with the Rogue River

Indians, who were hostile, restless and treacherous. Troops sent against them were frequently quartered in and around Canyonville, bringing considerable life to that quiet and isolated neighborhood. Sometimes wounded officers were brought there for rest and care. I well remember one handsome young captain, a graduate of West Point, who had been quite badly wounded in a skirmish with the Indians, and who was laid up with a crippled foot. I think this foot never did get entirely well. He had a young wife in the east who was dreadfully worried about him. Naturally enough. He used to read me some of her fine letters. He told me he had written her that his accident was a mere scratch, but it was far from being that. It seemed fairly criminal to me to see those splendid young men, all highly educated and often scions of fine families, sent out here in this wild country to battle with dastardly savages. Some of these young men lost their lives, and many others lost their health, fighting worthless, bloodthirsty redskins. The entire Indian population at that time did not seem to me to be worth the cost, the sacrifice of even one fine young man's life.

It was while we were at Canyonville that my second little daughter, Lillias, was born. She was a delicate little baby and required much careful attention. I spent most of my time looking after her.

And now, my globe-trotting husband had heard of another place that appealed to him strongly. We were about to move again. However, this was the beginning of the end of our moving. This time we were to be pioneers in the most primitive meaning of the word.

CHAPTER SEVEN

EARLY in the spring of 1853, a man named Perry B. Marple, a former minister of the gospel and a lawyer in one of the midwestern states, came into the Rogue River Valley on what he considered to be a mission of good will. Mr. Marple went up and down the Valley expatiating at length on the beauties and advantages of a region that lay far to the southwest, on the shore of the Pacific Ocean. This place was known as "Coos Bay."

A year or so earlier than this, Mr. Marple, with six other white men and two Indian guides, had visited this section. Since that time, he had been unable to forget what had seemed to him a veritable bit of Paradise. He had never relinquished the idea that some day it would be colonized and settled by white people.

Full of this dream, Mr. Marple came to our valley, where he discoursed eloquently to all that would listen, on the great future of this wonderful "Coos Bay country." Marple was an extremely visionary man, full of grand Utopian dreams. He really believed all he said about his new "discovery."

He was a fluent speaker and had little difficulty in drawing interested crowds of listeners around him as he talked in the streets of Jacksonville, a primitive little mining camp at that time, about this marvelous region. Everybody appeared to be interested in it. Mr. Marple undoubtedly drew a very alluring picture of this vast, unexplored region. It was not surprising that many were eager to see it. Mr. Marple offered to guide a party of strong, active young men to this favored locality, for a price, naturally. Many of the men that listened to Marple's glowing descriptions were adventurers, in a certain sense. Like ourselves, they had come to Oregon Territory to find wealth and success in life. Many of them, also like ourselves, were disappointed in their expectations and were looking for fresh fields that promised a richer, fuller harvest. The will o' the wisp beckoned them on.

Marple had no difficulty in organizing a party of forty hardy young men, my husband among them. Marple could have easily secured twice as many members, if he would have taken them. The avowed purpose of his company was to colonize and develop the Coos Bay country. Each member paid to Marple the sum of two hundred and fifty dollars for being the Moses to lead them to this new Promised Land, a land of glorious possibilities and advantages, they all believed. Since reaching the Far West, my husband had been disappointed and disillusioned in not finding the fabled "pot of gold" that he had expected to find at the end of the rainbow, otherwise, Oregon Territory.

Many other pioneers had similar experiences. In their judgment, this scheme of Mr. Marple's was the answer to their prayers. It provided the opportunity they had been seeking. In every detail it seemed to fit in with my husband's ideas, as well as his ideals. He hoped and fully expected to find in that region near the shore of the Pacific Ocean the place of his dreams and his desires. Mr. Marple had described the beautiful body of water that emptied into the ocean there and Freeman felt certain that Coos Bay was destined to be one of the world's great seaports.

Finally, after several busy weeks of preparation, all arrangements for the departure of the company were completed. No women were included in this party. If everything proved to be as rose-colored as Mr. Marple had declared it to be, the married men would soon return to the valley for their families.

My two babies and I waited patiently in our fairly comfortable quarters at Canyonville until we heard from my husband as to whether or not this new location had come up to his expectations. Finally a letter came, saying that everything was thoroughly satisfactory. The country was marvelous, the future assured.

He also wrote that only nineteen men of the original party of forty had gone on to Coos Bay. Soon after reaching the headwaters of the Coquille River, twenty-one of the men had expressed dissatisfaction at not finding gold, or even a trace of it. One small vein of coal had been found. With the consent of Mr. Marple, these discontented men left his party and returned to their valley homes.

After their departure, the remaining nineteen held a meeting, electing William H. Harris as their leader, thus displacing Mr. Marple, who was quite willing to relinquish his position. The name, "The Coos Bay Commercial Company," was adopted for the new organization.

The primary object of this company was to settle and develop the Coos Bay country, assist and civilize the natives and bring to the attention of the outside world the many advantages possessed by this vast new region. These were laudable ambitions indeed, but I might add here that few of them were realized. The company was to be a community or joint stock affair. All lands, mines or other property acquired by it were to be held in common. Each stockholder owned an equal number of shares. My husband also wrote that the new settlement, the future metropolis of that region, had been named "Empire City," a name suggestive of its great future.

Many other names had been suggested as the young pioneers lay around a great fire of driftwood one balmy June night, but all were rejected in favor of "Empire City." Freeman had written that he would be coming for us soon. Accordingly, the latter part of September—fortunately the weather was perfect at that time—my husband arrived to take us down to this wonderful new land. He said that this would be our home for all future time. We would move no more. Our wanderings were over. Freeman considered that the entire Coos Bay region possessed remarkable possibilities for great development. He declared that the splendid harbor there would bring commerce from all parts of the world.

Perhaps I was not quite so enthusiastic as he. I seemed to have heard all this before. I had moved too often since we had been in Oregon Territory to be very confident regarding any place I had not seen. However, I reserved my judgment until we had reached our destination. I knew it would be a strictly pioneer environment. I realized that there would be no luxuries of any kind, and probably few of the necessities. This was to be pioneering in the most primitive meaning of the word. Still, I did not dread it or shrink from it. It held a certain fascination for me. It seemed all a part of the game, as it were.

There was something mysterious, exciting and thrilling about going into an absolutely new country where white women had never before ventured. The thought fired my imagination. I hoped that it would prove to be all that my husband believed it to be, but I still had my doubts. In so far as the Indians were concerned, I felt no fear. My husband assured me that they were friendly. It was near the end of September before we finally started for our new home. The route my husband chose in returning to Coos Bay was entirely different from that which the members of the Marple expedition had taken. They had gone through Camas Valley, and after much devious wandering they had reached the headwaters of the Coquille River, had gone down that beautiful stream in Indian canoes, and after a stay of some days at the big Indian village at the mouth of the river, they had laboriously walked over the steep, rugged hills known as the "Seven Devils" to reach their destination.

It was a long and wearisome journey even for strong young men like themselves. This route would have been too strenuous a trip for women and little children. It would have been a dangerous one for them as well.

We rode on mules over the mountains, on trails that were steep, rough and narrow. My husband carried one of our children on his lap and I held my eight-months' old baby in the same way. It was often difficult for me to keep my seat on the mule. I thought many times that we were falling off his back.

In those days all women rode on side saddles, on one side of their mount only. This was really a most ridiculous fashion. It provided scant protection for the rider and was hard for both her and her animal. For a woman to ride astride, as they all do nowadays, would have been considered a most unwomanly and immodest thing to do. The woman that did this would have been almost disgraced in the eyes of many. You can understand that it was difficult for me to retain my precarious position on the mule with my baby on my lap. Fortunately, though, my animal was very sure-footed as mules usually are. Perhaps, too, he realized in some dim fashion that he was doing his bit in helping to settle the far west, and that made him more cautious.

At the time that my husband had returned for us, several other men from the Coos Bay colony also came back to the valley for their families. We thought it expedient to join company, for several reasons. With us were Dr. A. B. Overbeck, his wife and two little children, and Judge J. C. Tolman, with his family of two. All the children were practically babies. Both of these families rode as my husband and I did, each one with a child on their lap.

After much very hard riding, we reached Scottsburg, named for Levi Scott, of Portland, situated on the lovely Umpqua River about twenty-five miles from its mouth. A small settlement of white people was already there, and all most enthusiastic about the great future of their community. I might mention here that in December, 1861, after some days of torrential rains, a disastrous flood occurred there. The Umpqua River, like the Coquille and many other rivers in Oregon, swollen with water from melting snows, overflowed its banks, flooding the lower portion of the village and destroying much of it.

The fine new road that had been built at a cost of nearly fifty thousand dollars, and which had been constructed with great care, was almost entirely ruined. Scottsburg really never fully recovered from this blow.

At Scottsburg we embarked on the little river steamer *Washington*, the first steamboat of any kind ever to ply those placid waters. Coming down the river on the *Washington*, we passed the Curtis Noble family, also bound for Coos Bay.

They were obliged to travel somewhat slowly, as they had a scow, towed by a big Indian canoe, with a considerable load. They were bringing with them some cows, horses, pigs and chickens. This was the first livestock ever brought into Coos Bay, with the exception of horses and mules, which had come in with the first white men. We had probably been at Empire City about two weeks when the Nobles finally arrived.

In the following April, in 1854, Mrs. Noble gave birth to a daughter, whom they named "Emma." She was the first white child born in the county. I might add in this connection that the first white child born on the Coquille was "Annie," daughter of David J. and Marilla Ann Lowe.

When we arrived at Winchester Bay, at the mouth of the Umpqua, we again mounted our mules for the twenty-mile ride along the ocean beach to the settlement at Empire City, the future metropolis of the Golden West. I held my baby on my lap and my other little girl rode behind me, clinging tightly to a handkerchief tied around my waist. One might infer from this that my waist was not very large, when a handkerchief could encircle it. But the handkerchiefs were larger in those days than they are now, and my waist is also somewhat larger! The other two women of our party rode as I did, a child on the lap and another one behind. Our husbands led the mules, fearful lest they should take fright at the unaccustomed sights around them and dash into the surf with their precious burdens.

In this picturesque manner I made my first pilgrimage along the wave-washed shore of the mighty Pacific. This was my first glimpse of the ocean and I was tremendously impressed with it. It seemed so vast and powerful and incomprehensible. I felt as though it might at any moment roll up on the sands on which we were traveling and engulf us all. We seemed such tiny, infinitesimal atoms compared with it! We were absolutely helpless if a tidal wave should come. It made me rather nervous to contemplate all the dreadful things the ocean might do if it "took a notion." But of course nothing happened.

All went well with our small party of pioneer pilgrims. The day was beautiful and inspiring. The sun shone brilliantly, the blue waves glittered with a thousand points of dazzling light and the surf was low and white. All nature seemed propitious for our entry into our new home. Necessarily, we traveled at a very slow rate of speed. The mules never got out of a walk. Finally, after what seemed an interminable length of time, though we had enjoyed the novelty of our surroundings, we left the smooth ocean beach and started across the undulating sand hills to the other side, which was the Bay. We paused just about opposite where the town of Empire City now stands.

My husband said this was "the end of the trail" for us. I was not sorry to hear this, for riding for hours on the back of a very deliberate mule and caring for my babies at the same time had not been too joyous or comfortable. As my eyes first rested on the beautiful blue bay that flowed tranquilly along on its journey to the sea, my thoughts reverted to my childhood's home in the state of New York, on the shore of fair Cayuga Lake. It gave me a distinct feeling of homesickness, and I felt instinctively that I was going to like this new western country.

The people at the settlement had been expecting the arrival of the families, and soon after some loud shouting by our men, we perceived several large canoes coming across the bay. The stream here appeared to be a mile or more in width. The mules, greatly frightened and somewhat unruly, were finally induced to swim over, and before long we were all safely landed on the other side. Fortunately, it was a calm day. If it had been stormy, I do not know how we women would have enjoyed our first ride in an Indian canoe. It was really very beautiful where we landed on the other side, at the tiny settlement of Empire City. It was still in its wild, natural state, with splendid dark forests coming down almost to the water's edge.

It was about four o'clock in the afternoon of October 18, 1853, when we reached our journey's end. We went at once to the "hotel," a little log cabin, kept by genial Frank Ross. Here we feasted, literally, on fresh salmon, crabs, clams and roasted wild ducks and geese, all of which were delicious. Although we had to experiment somewhat with the shell-fish, we liked it from the first. This was fortunate for us, as it had to be a generous part of our future food supply.

That night we slept on a "puncheon" floor, in a big room with about forty other persons, both men and women, having only our own feather beds between us and the uneven logs of the floor. But we slept in peace and safety, lulled to rest by the sound of the surf beating musically on the ocean beach a few miles away.

The "city" of Empire at that time consisted of a few cabins and the "hotel," both built of logs in the usual primitive fashion. But all things must have a beginning, you know!

It is probable that we three were the first white women that had ever set foot in the Coos Bay country. It is more than likely that there were women and children among the seventy-five emigrants on the brig *Katie Heath*, which came into Coos Bay by mistake in 1850. However, it is not likely that they were allowed to go ashore, as the character of the natives was unknown at that time, and it was feared they might prove hostile. We have no record that any of the persons on this pioneer vessel ever went ashore. Apparently, we were the first white women that many of the Indians along our route had ever seen.

We certainly created a sensation among the male portion of the native population, especially among those on the lower Umpqua. These dirty, greasy creatures actually became offensive in their attention to us. My husband was a practical joker, and when he saw that the Indians were interested in us, he rather encouraged them, merely to have a little fun at their expense. But evidently, Indians have no sense of humor. They gazed at our white faces in undisguised admiration.

Anxiously and openly they besought our husbands to trade

wives with them. They offered all their blankets, their lovely
hand-woven baskets and matting, and their highly-prized
wampum, most of which belonged to their women, in addition to their dusky partners. When they were finally made
to understand that the white men could not accept their
offers, they put up their precious ponies, thinking that they
would clinch the bargain. But even then the strange palefaces were obdurate. They could not be induced to give up
their "white squaws."

In the distribution that had been made of the advan-
tageous points on and near the Bay to be held by the Coos
Bay Commercial Company, the high-sounding name of the
organization of the Marple party, my husband had been
assigned to the place now known as "North Bend," which
had no name whatever at that time. The present name was
given it by the late Captain Asa M. Simpson in 1856, because of the great north bend that the bay makes at or near
that point. An extremely large and valuable vein of coal was
supposed to exist at this place. My husband was put under
heavy bonds to hold it for his company, and he was supposed
to remain there and develop this great body of coal.

We stayed but one night at the metropolis—Empire City.
The following day I said a regretful goodbye to my pleasant
companions of the journey from the valley, and with my
husband and babies, and a man to assist with the moving, we
embarked on a little sloop owned jointly by my husband and
two others. We were going to our new home! I cannot say
that I was particularly thrilled or happy at the prospect. I
had been just a trifle disillusioned with Empire City, for
some unknown reason. I had expected to find things a little
different there. Though it was really very beautiful, just as
a kindly nature had made it, it was after all, absolutely nothing. I knew it would be extremely lonely for active young
women like Mrs. Tolman and Mrs. Overbeck. But still I
could almost find it in my heart to envy them because they
were to remain together, instead of going to a still more
remote location where they would be the only white women

among a tribe of Indians. "Empire City" was bad enough, but it seemed almost like Paradise when contrasted with the place where I was going.

However, Mrs. Tolman did not remain at Empire City very long. Judge Tolman, who had become a stockholder in the "Coos Bay Commercial Company," made some arrangement with the company by which he took over the place now known as Marshfield. He had two log cabins, or one double one, built, to be ready for occupancy soon after his return to the Bay with us. There he took his little family. He did a considerable trade with the Indians and the few white settlers near there. However after the lapse of a year or so, Mrs. Tolmon's health failed and the family returned to their valley home.

But as to ourselves; I must confess that I looked forward to our new location with considerable curiosity, not unmixed with trepidation, though I felt no fear whatsoever regarding the Indians. I was a pioneer wife and mother and I thought I could endure anything that my husband could. I felt that I had resources within myself. I had some of my beloved books with me, and I planned to resume my study of French, which had been sadly neglected since my arrival in Oregon Territory. Then, too, I had my botany, a relic of dear old school days at Norwalk Academy, and I visioned the pleasure I would have in discovering and classifying new flowers and shrubs. Before leaving Canyonville my husband had sent most of our household goods to Empire City by packers. These things together with others, were already awaiting us upon our arrival.

A brisk sea breeze filled the sails of our staunch little craft and we rapidly covered the intervening five or six miles between Empire City and our future home. This was my first ride in a sail boat and I was just a trifle terrified, especially when the sail would "jibe." But it was all interesting and held a strange fascination for me. It was so unlike anything I had ever before experienced.

As we rounded the point immediately below North Bend

and our sloop came in view of the natives, they began coming down to the water's edge to greet us. By the time we were tied up at our landing, scores of them had arrived. Whether or not they were pleased to see us, I did not know. Their immobile countenances gave no indication of their feelings. More natives appeared. Presently, there seemed to be hundreds of them. I could not call this a "royal" welcome, exactly, for I did not know what the Indians were thinking about. But I sincerely hoped that their thoughts of us were pleasant ones!

They followed us up to the little one-room cabins that had been built for us in the almost unbroken forests. Several of them helped my husband and the man to carry some of the heavier things up the hill to the cabins. Certainly everything seemed peaceful. Soon we had our belongings disposed as best we could.

I had to admit that my stout heart quailed a little as I looked around me. The view from our cabins was superb— a wide expanse of blue water, and dark wooded hills in the distance. Each time I glanced at the sparkling bay I thought of my dear old home on fair Cayuga Lake. But this recollection brought me scant comfort.

The place seemed literally to teem with Indians, big and little, old and young, good-looking and otherwise, all sorts and conditions of them. That neighborhood was apparently a favorite place or home for them.

Gradually, as the days passed, I thought less and less about them. I ceased to worry and accepted them as a sort of necessary evil. They were apparently friendly. Of course it was not exactly agreeable to have so many of them around constantly, but we paid no special attention to them. We simply took them for granted, as being a part of our new life that we had no power to alter.

As I had been traveling almost constantly for nearly three weeks and had been unable to launder any clothes during that time, I soon did a very large family washing. This I hung out on the many bushes around my cabin door. Everything was of course very inconvenient for the process of washing and it was late before I finished. As the day was short and dark, by dusk the clothes were not dry, so I concluded to leave them out until the sun could shine on them the following day.

But guess what happened! When I arose the next morning and looked out, my dismay may perhaps be imagined when I saw that all my clothes were gone—stolen by those thieving Indians! At first glance I thought there was something wrong with my vision; that I was not seeing things right. But my eyes had not deceived me. Every article of clothing was gone.

I never regained a single piece of my sorely-needed garments in that isolated region. The rascally natives had taken advantage of this grand opportunity to replenish their very scanty wardrobes at our expense. Later, at various times, I saw some of my handkerchiefs and towels wound around the squaws' greasy necks, but I never dared to mention this trifling little matter to them.

Although the theft of the washing was a near-tragedy to us, I have often thought since of what a joy and a wild frolic the whole proceeding must have seemed to the natives themselves. While we were slumbering peacefully in our little log cabin in that great, silent forest, they were stepping furtively about, stealthily lifting our clothes from the bushes. I can imagine with what grunts of satisfaction they fitted my babies' clothes on their own dusky offspring the following day, how the braves robed themselves in my husband's underwear and how the dirty squaws put on my dainty house dresses. What a new, rich experience for these simple, ignorant people! They must have thought that the Great Spirit had sent rare gifts to them.

Fortunately, I had a bolt of domestic (we call it "muslin" nowadays) among our stores. I had to go right to work making some new clothes for my little ones. This was no small task in those days, before sewing machines were in use, or maybe not yet invented. The loss of the clothes was really a serious one to us. Many of the stolen articles we could not replace at that time.

For the first few weeks all went smoothly enough, if we may except the theft of the "washing." The Indians were friendly, too friendly, in fact, for their calls at the cabin with requests for food became too frequent. I did not dare to refuse their demands, for I realized that we were in their power. Still, we did not fear them. Gradually, however, there came muttering of discontent from among them.

They looked on us with jealous eyes, declaring that we had stolen their "illahee" (land). My husband dug up some ground near the cabins and planted a few potatoes, thinking that in this mild climate they would grow all winter and thus help to solve the problem of providing fresh vegetables for us. Some of the natives were interested spectators of the potato planting, and a little later, when they had commenced to come up, the Indians came at night and dug up every potato.

They were gradually getting a little too free with everything we had. Matters began to look somewhat ominous. Finally, one warm Sunday afternoon, about six weeks after our arrival, a band of fifty or sixty natives, in war paint and feathers, armed with bows and arrows, came to our cabins in a sullen, quiet demonstration. They were led by an old chief, with a young Umpqua Indian as interpreter. Their quiet demeanor was soon broken. In loud, angry tones they demanded, and commanded too, that we give up everything we had there and leave the place at once. We had no right there, they declared. Among other bad things we were doing, we were frightening the fish away from the streams. Already there were fewer elk and deer in the forests, fewer ducks and geese on the marshes, fewer berries in the woods because of our presence.

Soon there would be nothing left for the Indians. The white men would own everything, they said. My husband was not at all excited or alarmed over their threats. To him, the natives were merely a lot of foolish, ignorant, prejudiced children. They really did not know what they wanted. This he knew, and he proceeded to tell them all about it.

Freeman was always very brave when a crisis occurred and never seemed to lose his head. He had seen the little cavalcade marching along to our door and had come outside to meet them. He listened silently and respectfully to all they had to say, never once interrupting them. He let them talk as long as they wished. When they had finished speaking, Freeman quietly buckled his revolver about his waist, mounted a large stump standing near and began addressing them. They seemed to accord him the same courtesy he had shown them, and for a time were hushed and silent. But as he proceeded, there came occasionally grunts of disapproval. But Freeman paid no attention to these.

I listened to him, and saw the effect of his words. The memory of the old Ohio days when he used to mesmerize some of his audience, came back to me. I wondered if he had regained some of his lost "power" and was using it on these unfriendly savages. He had by this time learned much of the native jargon and could make himself fairly well understood without much aid from the interpreter. Probably this knowledge of their language had a mollifying effect upon the crowd. He began in a calm, low voice, telling the excited throng that we had come there to stay, that we wanted to help the natives in every way that we could. He told them we would improve the land so that the whole country would be better and richer; that we would teach their people many useful things that they would be glad to know, and that we would always be the Indians' friend.

All the natives had a great respect for "Uncle Sam," as they designated the United States, and Freeman told them that the Great White Father at Washington, the President of the United States, had told the white men to come and live there and help the Indians to a better way of living. Freeman told them it was their duty, as good Indians, to help their country to be big and powerful, the finest country in all the world. Then, it would be known everywhere for its fine, splendid natives. He appealed to their pride in their race, to their imagination to vision the future that lay before them with the help of the friendly white man. Much more he told them, in simple, eloquent language that they all seemed to understand.

After considerable parleying on both sides, with some apparent objectors in the crowd, Freeman at last succeeded in pacifying them, so that they said we might continue to stay there, but no other white people could come, they declared positively. The entire place belonged to the red men, they said. It had always been theirs and they would keep it for their own people.

The truce, however, was but a short-lived one. Within a few days, they were as hostile as before. Numbers of them would lounge around our cabins, lean familiarly over the ledge of the opening that served as a window, and point meaningly to the goods and provisions on our rough shelves. Then, with significant looks and gestures, they would discuss the matter among themselves. Of course I could always imagine they were telling each other that all these things would soon be theirs, and were even then selecting their own favorite articles from the lot.

As it later developed, this was exactly what they were doing. Within a week after the big "pow-wow," they were once more literally "on the war path." At this critical juncture we had in our employ a man named Connor, a good-hearted, kindly fellow, but inclined to be very much afraid of the Indians. Not without good reason, too. For some time he had feared violence from them. Somehow, we had not felt that way. Connor said the natives "were up to mischief," of that he felt certain.

One day, about this time, as Connor was cutting stove wood for me near the cabins, he had two other men from Empire City visiting him for a few hours. As the men chatted idly together there, a number of naked Indians suddenly appeared in their midst. The fact that the natives were entirely nude was in itself rather an alarming circumstance.

Usually, they wore some clothing, if only the skin of a wild animal. In a mixture of English and jargon these Indians informed Connor and his companions that they would be called upon the following night to go to the Indians' huts. They were sternly told not to disobey the summons. At this, Connor turned white with fear. The intruders instantly perceived this. Stepping towards the terrified man, one Indian stripped open Connor's shirt with a quick, insolent gesture. Placing his hand upon the frightened white man's breast, he felt the beating of his heart.

"Ni-ka tum-tum hyui wa-wa!" (Your heart talks very loud!) he said, scornfully.

Giving the three men each an Indian name and again warning them to come when they were called by three knocks on their cabin door the next night, the natives departed as silently as they had appeared.

I had been a listener to this strange and very disturbing conversation and was naturally much concerned over it. In a few minutes Connor and the other men entered my cabin, relating the details of the incident and urging me to get into their canoe with my children immediately and hasten to Empire City with them. My inclinations urged me strongly to do this. I realized now that danger was near us all. But duty was stronger than inclination.

My husband had gone down to the settlement the day before to attend a company meeting and I felt positive that he would return that evening. By this time I had seen so much of Indians and their stupid actions that I really did not have much fear of them. I considered them arrant cowards, what we would call "bluffers" nowadays. But I had to admit to myself that it did look like real business now.

In those little cabins in the unfriendly wilderness we had what we considered to be large stores of provisions, such as flour, sugar, bacon, molasses, beans and other staples. I knew that we could not afford to give them up to the Indians without at least a struggle to retain them, especially as such supplies could not be obtained anywhere on the bay at that

time. Practically all of our worldly goods were contained
in those tiny cabins, as we had invested between fifteen hundred and two thousand dollars in supplies.

We expected that we would occasionally make a trade with
either the white settlers or the natives. So, after deliberating,
1 decided to remain there until evening, anyway. I agreed
that if my husband had not returned by then, I would go
down to Empire City with Connor, whose two friends had
already departed hurriedly.

Connor stayed with me, much against his better judgment,
I know, but he would not desert a helpless woman and her
babies in such an extremity. I assure you that I fully appreciate his chivalry. What would I have done without him?
We both realized that a crisis had at last been reached. While
waiting for my husband's return, Connor and I busied ourselves packing up everything preparatory to a sudden departure. No Indians appeared all that afternoon. This was
an ominous sign, but we were thankful for their absence.
Probably if they had seen our preparations for leaving, they
would not have permitted us to proceed. They wanted our
goods, there was no doubt about that. Though the day was
short, it seemed like an eternity to both Connor and myself
until eight o'clock that night, when Freeman finally arrived.

After listening to a hurried recital of the day's events, he
began preparing for an immediate departure. He realized
now that the end of our stay there had come—the Indians
were victorious at last. It was useless to attempt resistance.
We must accept the verdict and get away as soon as possible,
even if we had to leave all our belongings behind. Our own
personal safety must come first. I really think Freeman felt
that it was somewhat doubtful if we would be allowed to
leave, but he did not express this doubt to me then.

The staunch little sloop that had brought me to this inhospitable home a few weeks earlier, and in which my husband
had returned that evening, lay at anchor below. In that
pitch-black night, not knowing whether the Indians were
watching us or not, and if they planned an attack upon us if

we attempted to leave, our goods were hastily but very quietly transferred to the boat. This work consumed some time, though everything was ready to be taken away immediately. The long, rather slow task was finally accomplished. Things were safely stowed away on the sloop. Then the sleeping babies, happily unconscious of impending danger, were carried down by their father and Connor. I had my arms full of small things I had gathered up almost at the last minute.

Day was just breaking as we boarded the sloop and stood out into the bay, bound for a place of safety for ourselves and our little ones. As we glided away from the unfriendly shore, some of the natives saw us, and giving the alarm, a crowd of them came rushing down to the bank.

"Mika klatawa," (You going), they cried in amazement.

"Yes," we answered lightly, "Nika klatawa" (We are going). "Kla-how-ya!" (Good-bye!)

A shower of arrows whizzed through the air, but they fell harmlessly into the water near by.

Through all that perilous few minutes, I still remember the beauty of that early morning. The dawn was coming up, the sky was beginning to redden, the quiet waters of the bay were rippling with irridescent light. Somehow, these sights imprinted themselves upon my mind indelibly.

Two hours later we were safe at Empire City. We felt that we had much for which to be thankful. The little settlement looked very good to me now. I was genuinely glad to be there. Later, we learned that the Indians had planned a general massacre of all the white people in the bay region. This was only prevented by the advice of a California half-breed named Sam.

He sagely told the natives that they had waited a little too long to accomplish this plan successfully. Sam had said to them, "If you wanted to kill these people, you should have done so as they came into your country a few at a time. Then you could have managed it all right. But now it is too late. There are many white men here. If you killed all of them, or one of them, Uncle Sam would hear about it. He would send his Boston soldiers down here with very many big guns. They would not leave one Indian alive. Even the women and children might be killed!"

So we had actually come close to tragedy. The natives were wise enough to take Sam's good advice. Thus, for the second time, our lives had been saved by a half-breed. Since that time, I have had a very high regard for these people.

CHAPTER EIGHT

WE found considerable change in the little settlement we had left scarcely two months before. Comfortable log cabins had sprung up here and there in the forests, built by adventurous people who, like ourselves, had been lured to this locality with tales of its marvelous richness. The place really seemed quite civilized, perhaps more so than it actually was because of comparison with the place we had just left.

Everybody felt the need of closer communication with the outside world. We were completely isolated, far from any settlement of white people. We had been told that soon ships would be entering our splendid harbor, and we waited anxiously for the first one to arrive. Lieutenant McArthur, in the United States schooner *Ewing* had surveyed our bar from the outside, only in a hurried, somewhat superficial manner, but he had reported that it would permit the entrance of steamers. Therefore, when in the early spring of 1854, a sail was seen outside the harbor, the joyful intelligence quickly spread throughout the settlement.

The long-expected ship, bringing supplies, provisions and men to work in the mines, had at last arrived! Eager to welcome the boat, her passengers and crew, six venturesome men of the village hastily manned a big canoe and went boldly and gaily out to the heaving bar. But they were all landsmen who did not thoroughly understand managing their clumsy craft, which was soon overturned by the turbulent waves and all its occupants drowned. This deplorable accident cast widespread gloom over the little village for a time. It was the first tragedy of its kind to occur there, and it could not be forgotten easily in our small community. Aside from the loss of the men living in our midst, who were sorely needed in this new country, it seemed a bad omen for the future of our shipping. Mr. Henry Stark, one of the lost men, had been a member of the original Coos Bay Commercial Company. I believe the name of the ship they were attempting to welcome was the *Cynosure,* commanded by Captain Whippey.

A short time before this, great excitement had been created in our midst by the discovery of gold in considerable quantities at Randolph "diggings," about twenty-eight miles or so down the beach from Empire City. So high became the fever of speculation and the desire for speedy riches that practically everybody deserted Empire City and rushed to the new gold mines. Of course all expected to make their fortunes picking up the golden nuggets from the Randolph beaches. My husband, a born speculator, had been among the first to rush into the new "diggings." Most of the men walked over from Empire City, the lucky ones carrying their supplies and mining equipment on pack-mules. Those not so fortunate carried their belongings on their backs.

At first there was no accommodation whatever at Randolph for women and children. I waited for my husband to get a little cabin built for us and it was not until April, 1854, that we ventured to go over to the mines. Mrs. Dean, a neighbor, whose husband had also joined the rush, accompanied us with her little family. We went up the bay in a large canoe as far as the Isthmus, then through Beaver Slough to the Coquille River and on down to Randolph. I am positive that we two were the first white women ever to go through, or over that historic waterway, then known as Beaver Slough.

Randolph was a very busy little mining town for a brief time, with about a thousand inhabitants, mostly men, who had come from different parts of the Territory in a mad rush for the precious yellow metal. It is really amazing how the news of a big gold "strike" travels. In no time at all, the world seems to know about it. At Randolph the ocean beach was staked off into "claims" for miles, and rough boarding houses and log cabins sprang up like magic. Of course, all the activities of a frontier mining camp flourished, including the dance hall, the saloon and the poker table, where the gambler played with his cocked revolver beside him.

The new mines did not prove as rich as had been expected, though several men made fortunes there. It was said that two brothers took out one hundred and fifty thousand dollars' worth of gold dust and nuggets, and another man carried out a mule-load of gold dust, valued at eighty thousand dollars.

Soon winter came, with its fierce storms and high, tempestuous tides, obliterating all the "claims," and by the time spring had returned, the golden sands were scattered and covered by cold gray valueless sands. The disappointed fortune-seekers went sadly back to their little abandoned homes. There are many stretches of these rich black sands scattered along, or near the Oregon coasts. Some of them are located several miles inland, where the ocean beach used to be. These deposits are supposed to be the richest of all. The gold itself is very fine, what has been called "flour" gold, in most infinitesimal flakes or scales, so fine and small that thus far there has never been a machine or process invented that will separate the gold from the sand profitably. But some day, when a process is discovered, vast fortunes will be made from the same old black sands where many persons spent small fortunes in a vain effort to acquire wealth.

My husband at one time owned a mine known as the Eagle Black Sand Mine, and once we had high hopes of selling this mine for one hundred and fifty thousand dollars. I remember that some of the capitalists interested in the business came up from San Francisco to look over the property. They stopped in Empire City, which was then about the only place that could provide comfortable quarters.

They personally inspected the mine they expected to purchase; some of the men interested were James Fair, Seth Cook, John Mackey and James Morgan, all very prominent in the financial world of the Pacific Coast at that time. Little Empire City was quite set up over its distinguished visitors, who seemed satisfied with their prospective purchase. Unfortunately, though, the new secret process that had been discovered and which was depended upon to save the gold proved, like all those preceding it, and those that followed it as well, to be a failure.

Thus vanished our dream of wealth! Occasionally, as the years passed, we had prospects of disposing of the mine for a considerable sum, but these prospects always came to naught after investigation.

My husband, who had made a scientific study of the contents of the sand, in so far as a layman could do it, always maintained that in addition to gold, silver and platinum found in these black sands, there were many other valuable minerals. Nowadays, analyses of assayers are confirming his opinion and declare that radium, serpentine, chrome, magnetic iron and many other minerals are present in the rich black sands of the ancient ocean beaches.

With the exodus from Randolph largely located in Empire City, the place began to assume quite a cosmopolitan air. Messrs. Northrup and Simonds, from Portland, Oregon, merchants and capitalists, had by this time become interested in the extensive coal deposits at Newport, as the place at the head of Coal Bank Slough was called. These men established a general merchandise store at Empire City, which thus became the depot of supplies for the whole country.

Thus far the sanguine hopes of the Coos Bay Commercial Company had not been realized. Coal of sufficiently good quality for shipment to outside markets had not yet been found, owing to the fact the miners had not yet had time to penetrate sufficiently far below the surface to find good coal. However, as coal was selling for forty dollars a ton in San Francisco, an attempt was made to send a cargo of it there. But the old brig *Chancey*, on which the coal was shipped, was wrecked going out over the Coos Bay bar and the project ended in disaster and disappointment. Finally, as a result of continued failures and disappointments, the great Coos Bay Commercial Company was dissolved.

Naturally, provisions continued scarce and high but owing to kindly nature's bountiful supply of fish, shell-fish, wild game of many kinds, and berries, no actual want was ever felt. "When the tide was out, the table was spread."

Milk was scarce and sold for one dollar a gallon, skim milk at that. Eggs were a dollar and a quarter a dozen, and scarce as hen's teeth. We were glad to get them at any price. Once my husband had an opportunity to buy a keg of ten dozen eggs, and I looked forward with pleasant anticipation to having some cakes and cookies, as well as other things that required eggs in their making. But our neighbors also wanted eggs, and begged so hard for some that we let them have all but two dozen at the same price we had paid for them—a dollar and a quarter a dozen. Potatoes and onions, old, sprouted and half-decayed, were twenty cents a pound. Dried apples and peaches were the same price. Flour, often mouldy, and sometimes wormy, was ten dollars for a fifty-pound sack.

I remember hearing some of the pioneers tell of an experience they had before the arrival of any woman or children. They had grown tired of living on clams, crabs, wild game and fish, and wanted some "real" meat, either beef or pork. Therefore, they chartered a sloop in the harbor to go to the Umpqua and bring them down a supply of the desired meat, as well as some other needed supplies. But the bar was "solleks" (angry, rough), and the boat could not cross out. In this emergency, the natives were appealed to, and soon they appeared with a quantity of meat which they told the men was "salt chuck chusha," which interpreted into English means "salt water pork," or "corned" pork. The meat was very good and the men enjoyed it for about two weeks, until they discovered that what they had been eating and enjoying was seal meat, instead of pork.

Naturally, we suffered many privations, but we expected that and did not complain. Our lights were all home-made tallow "dips." We had no beef in those days, but we had more than an abundance of elk and deer, and we made our candles from their suet. I fancy there are not many persons in the world today that ever saw or used elk-tallow candles!

We never really suffered for lack of good food, either, though we did not always have exactly what we wanted. With the great variety of sea-food, wild fowl and wild game of which I have already spoken, we also had a considerable variety of wild fruit, among these being blackberries, salmonberries, thimble berries, gooseberries, raspberries and later in the season red and black huckleberries. The blackberries were especially delicious. They were similar to our dewberries at home. I used to dry quantities of these fruits for winter use. Practically all of them were of a superior quality.

The Indians always seemed to enjoy supplying the white people with sea-food, wild game and berries, in those days rarely appearing to want money for their wares. They much preferred to have some of the newcomers' clothing or some other article from the belongings of the palefaces.

Even fifteen years from the time of which I speak, all the things the Indians brought us were ridiculously cheap. I think the natives, as a rule, were very honest people. They seemed absolutely free from guile or deceit. I remember that "Ticky Tom," a fine, upright fellow, used to bring me ducks and geese throughout the seasons in the '70's, all beautifully dressed and cleaned, made ready for the oven, by his neat little wife Kate. The ducks brought one dollar a dozen, and the geese twenty-five cents each. But those days are gone forever from this part of the world!

I recall an incident that occurred in connection with the early settlement here that might have had far-reaching and serious consequences for the future of this community. The old steamer *Newport* was the first steam vessel, so far as I know, to enter the harbor in 1856. I believe it was employed in carrying coal from the Newport mines to San Francisco, also freight and passengers. On one of her early trips, her owner and manager, General Estell, who was also superintendent of the California State Prison, was requested to send up a few laborers for the coal mines. The superintendent was a kindly man and anxious to assist the unfortunate men under his charge. It probably occurred to him that here was a chance to give some of them the opportunity of leading a new life among strangers that knew nothing of their past.

Accordingly, he selected those he deemed most suitable for the work and worthy of assistance and when the *Newport* made her next appearance in Coos Bay waters she brought with her forty ex-convicts. Some of these men went on with the steamer to the mines in the upper bay, but the majority of them stopped at Empire City. Of course we were all ignorant concerning the character of these men and had no knowledge of their former history.

But our eyes were soon opened. Heretofore, there had been no thievery in the settlement. Everything was safe, even when left outside indefinitely. But now a change came o'er the scene. At night, our clothes' lines were denuded of our husbands' garments. Our chicken houses were robbed of fowls and eggs. Everything of use or value not well protected, mysteriously disappeared. We looked at each other wonderingly. Gradually, the truth dawned upon our unsuspecting minds. We realized that we had a nest of robbers in our midst.

The citizens rose in righteous wrath and ordered these undesirables to return to California on the same boat that brought them. They did not dare disobey, for our men were stern and unyielding. Thereafter, we were left in peace. Although many years have passed since that time, to this day, whenever these unwelcome guests are mentioned, they are always referred to as "The Forty Thieves."

It was during the first year or so after our arrival on Coos Bay that a frightful accident occurred that is almost without a parallel in the history of the entire country. John Yoakam, a newcomer, with his wife and seven children, the oldest a girl of fourteen years, had located a claim in the unbroken forest about six miles from Empire City near what is now known as the "Old Cammann Road." They had built a little log cabin on the place where they lived happily, dreaming of the time when they would make their home in the wilderness blossom as the rose, for they were young and ambitious and did not spare their strength.

For some time they had been busily engaged in felling timber and burning trees that were uncomfortably near their cabin. At the time of the accident, they had a number of trees on fire. One very large tree, a patriarch of the forest, not far distant, had caused them some uneasiness, but after a careful examination of it one evening about nine o'clock, both Mr. and Mrs. Yoakam decided that there was no probability that the tree would fall that night. They felt certain, however, that if by any remote chance the tree should fall, it would not be in the direction of their cabin.

It was a cold, rainy night in March. A fitful wind tossed the branches of the trees wildly but the seven little children slumbered peacefully in their beds, happily unconscious of the dreadful fate that was so soon to overtake most of them. Hardly had Mr. and Mrs. Yoakam re-entered their cabin after their inspection of the burning tree, ere a fearful sound of splitting and crackling timber was heard. The husband and father realized instantly what had occurred. The great tree was falling!

"Run for your lives," he shouted. "The tree is falling on the house!"

The four older children, roused from sleep by the cries of their father, rushed for the open door, followed by their father. The mother paused, to snatch her baby from its cradle and at that moment the treacherous tree fell with a terrific crash upon the little cabin, shattering it completely.

As the tree descended upon the house, its heavy limbs caught and entangled the four children, killing them almost instantly. A branch struck the mother, injuring her arm and shoulder but she did not think of her own pain. Her anxious heart was with her hapless little ones. It was not until she reached the light from the burning stumps near her ruined home that she discovered the child she held in her arms was dead.

When the first horror and agony of the situation had

passed, the anguished parents searched for their two little boys, Jasper and John, aged six and four years, who had not escaped from the shattered cabin. They expected to find only their maimed and mangled bodies, but to their inexpressible joy, they found them in their little trundle-bed alive, unharmed and still fast asleep! The branches of the tree had fallen in such a manner as to completely shield their bed and the commotion had not even awakened them.

All that long, dreadful night the broken-hearted parents worked to extricate their dead children from the enveloping branches of the faithless tree.

As soon as morning dawned, the father hastened to Empire City and told us of the awful disaster that had befallen them. After listening to his pathetic story, a number of us women purchased a quantity of soft, fine, white cambric and accompanied him to the claim, where we spent the day making shrouds for the unfortunate children.

I shall never forget the solemn sadness of that final scene, the five small white-robed bodies lying in a row, snatched from life and its joys almost literally in the twinkling of an eye. The unhappy parents never rebuilt their cabin. They abandoned their claim in the unfriendly forest and sought a new home in a more congenial and fertile spot.

Many, many years have passed since that fatal night, but the place is still deserted. No one has ever made it his habitation or his home. It is known as "Yoakam's Hill." The merciless elements have long since obliterated the graves of the little sleepers, but over them the tall firs and cedars wave their evergreen branches in ceaseless requiem for those that lie below. But this is a sad tale and to make amends I will relate one of an entirely different nature, although to one of the principals in this story it was akin to a tragedy.

In the early days of the settlement's history, there was, naturally enough, a great surplus of bachelors of all sorts and conditions, ranging in ages from twenty to sixty years. There was a corresponding scarcity of young women, that is, young white ones. There were numbers of dusky maidens of the forest, many of them very beautiful girls, and to these some of the aforesaid bachelors paid ardent and continuous court.

Under the existing conditions, it may be imagined, perhaps, how the hearts of the lonely swains were set all a'flutter one day by the arrival of a man and his wife, accompanied by their niece, whom we will call Miss Caroline. She was a dainty, pretty blonde of "sweet sixteen." Of course, she was immediately besieged with attentions, all of which she accepted with apparent delight. There was a constant program of boat-rides, walks, picnics, dances. There were also countless gifts of furs, baskets, beads, arrowheads, choice fish and clams, haunches of venison, wild fowl, and everything fine that the country afforded. Miss Caroline took all these things as a queen might accept gifts from her loyal subjects. She possessed the faculty of making each cavalier believe that he was especially favored by her. She was a born coquette. It was as natural for her to flirt as it was for her to breathe, and for aught I know she was as innocent of her coquetry as she was of her breathing.

The happy months sped by, the suitors one and all under a spell. Suddenly a bomb was thrown into their midst by the announcement that Miss Caroline's aunt and uncle were to return east and that she was to go with them! Consternation reigned in the ranks of the faithful. The young lady was immediately deluged with applications for private interviews and long walks with one only, but she turned a deaf ear to the pleadings, excusing herself by saying that she was too busy with preparations for departure to spare the time.

Among her train was a fairly-young ex-sea captain, a pleasant, sensible fellow, ordinarily, who had come to Coos Bay seeking his fortune. He had been especially attentive to Miss Caroline and apparently she had given him reason to believe that she regarded him most favorably. Several days before her intended departure, he came to me in some embarrassment. He finally told me that he was going to be married and he begged me, as a very great favor, to furnish him and his bride with room and board until such time as he could get a little house built. Of course I had plenty of work as it was, with my little family and teaching school besides, but the poor man was so insistent and appeared so worried that I did not have the heart to refuse him.

He said he was to accompany Miss Caroline to the Umpqua when she left Empire City, and that he would bring her back as his wife. He added that she had not yet given him a positive answer but that she had promised to do so when they reached the Umpqua and he was certain it would be a favorable one. At last the eventful day of departure arrived. The ex-captain went with the party as he had said he intended doing, and several other anxious and hopeful suitors also went along!

About three days later, I heard a timid knock at my door. Opening it, I saw the would-be bridegroom standing there alone. No golden-haired bride was with him. A look of deep dejection was on his usually sunny countenance. He asked me abruptly if he could go to the room he had engaged and when I told him that he could, he staggered in and disappeared. I saw no more of him that day. After twenty-four hours of silence on his part, I became somewhat alarmed and, rapping lightly on his door, I heard a faint voice say "Come in!" I entered and found the man in bed, weak and feverish and quite ill. I began doctoring him immediately, but he had no heart for anything—not even for getting well. All the dainties I prepared for him I brought away almost untouched.

At last he told me the story. Miss Caroline had kept her promise at the Umpqua. She had given him the interview he had so long desired, and he was told in the briefest, coldest manner possible that she had never for an instant contemplated marrying him or any other man in this heathenish country. She said she would not accept the entire region as a gift if she had to live in it as one of the conditions of acceptance. She thanked him for the good times he had given her but she could not understand why he had even dreamed that there was anything serious about the whole affair.

The poor fellow remained in bed for three days and from that time he was a changed man. I often wondered later, as I saw this broken-hearted chap going about, if Miss Caroline ever realized how cruel she had been. Perhaps the time came when she bitterly repented for her conduct here. She never returned to the Bay, so I had no opportunity to learn of her future. I trust, however, that she developed into a good woman. Young people are not often intentionally cruel. They simply do not think about consequences. "You cannot put an old head on young shoulders," is a true saying.

Another interesting pioneer experience concerned a little red hen, a very unusual fowl, I thought then and still think. In the spring of our second year in Empire City, I was fortunate enough to buy a pair of half grown chickens, paying three dollars for the two.

In three months the little pullet began to lay and you can imagine the excitement that pervaded our entire household when she deposited her first small white egg in the barrel I had provided for that purpose. This wonderful little creature seemed to realize the value and scarcity of eggs and chickens, for she continued to lay until she had thirteen pretty white eggs in the nest. Then she proceeded to sit on them in regulation hen style and in due time she brought out thirteen downy chickens. In exactly three weeks from that time she "weaned" her babies and began to lay again, this time not stopping until she had fifteen eggs in her nest. Then she again began setting and again hatched every egg. But still this industrious little hen was not satisfied. In a few weeks she repeated her former exploits, this time laying seventeen eggs, every one of which she successfully hatched and reared every chick to maturity. It seemed to me that this was a record even for a pioneer hen. That summer I raised sixty chickens besides using manv eggs and fowls for the table, and I can truthfully say that we thoroughly appreciated them.

Speaking of chickens reminds me of an incident akin to tragedy, that occurred in the early days when chickens were almost an unknown quantity on the Bay. You can understand that amusements in the village were limited in their nature and variety. We women had our quilting bees and our little sewing parties but there was no "bridge" playing in those days. The only place where the men and women could mingle together socially was at a "ball" and of course they were very popular although not very frequent. There was none of your modern fancy dancing then, no "jazz" or "tango" or "rumba," but good old-fashioned, clean, wholesome quadrilles, where you had a chance to visit with your partner occasionally. Decorous waltzes, polkas, mazurkas and schottisches were interspersed with the graceful quadrilles.

A big room over the "store" was used for the dances, and tallow candles furnished the necessary light.

Washington's Birthday was approaching and it was planned to give a grand ball upon this occasion. The midnight supper that invariably accompanied these parties was to be the special feature of the affair and to make this unusually momentous the committee having the supper in charge, sent to Scottsburg, forty miles away and at great expense, for three dozen chickens.

In due time the fowls arrived, killed and dressed, having had quite an eventful journey. They were immediately turned over to a certain dear friend of ours, a charming woman, who had the well-deserved reputation of being a fine cook. She was instructed to make chicken pies for the big supper. There was much eager anticipation in regard to these pies, for none of us had tasted such dainties since coming to the Bay. We had wild duck and venison pies occasionally but they did not take the place of our good old-fashioned chicken pies.

The night of the ball arrived. The banquet was spread, the guests seated. I remember the scene perfectly after all these years. Long tables had been set out and near the head

of one sat the maker of the pies, surrounded by a small crowd
of friends, myself among them.

With many a merry laugh and jest going around, the
gentleman at the extreme end of our table carefully cut into
the golden-brown pie placed before him and with a courtly
inclination of the head, handed a plate of it to the lady sitting
next to him. And thus the serving went on, until all had
been supplied. We all watched the ceremony with great interest. Finally the last guest had been served. Expectantly,
then, we took up our forks, anxious to taste this longed-for
delicacy. But a familiar and unmistakable odor assailed our
nostrils. As each one tasted the pie he lifted his eyes in
horrified surprise. We looked wonderingly at each other,
mutely asking the questions we did not dare to put into
words. The chicken was simply "impossible."

Generally we had some very hot weather in February, as
we frequently have now, and the past few days had been
unusually warm. The long journey in the hot sun with its
many necessary changes had been ruinous to the fowls. Still
not a word was spoken. The silence became positively pain-
ful. Suddenly, the maker of the pies, deeply embarrassed,
her face flushed, rose to her feet. For a moment she looked
as though she was about to speak. But instead she burst into
tears and fled from the room. I followed her in a few moments and found her still in tears, quite broken-hearted over
what she termed the "calamity" concerning the chicken pies.

She said she had realized the condition of the fowls before
they were cooked, but she hoped that with the high seasoning
she had used, besides the rich gravy and the pie crust, that
the disagreeable odor and taste would not be apparent. It
was quite pathetic to see her grief and chagrin. The time
never came when she could discuss the matter without emotion, though the rest of us considered the whole thing a
prodigious joke. But my friend felt that she had in some
way disgraced herself in the eyes of her fellow townsfolk.

About this time I had an opportunity to buy four baby
pigs. This seemed to me a fine chance to add bacon and ham

to our rather limited larder. I bought the pigs, paying ten dollars for the quartet. They grew and thrived amazingly as all little pigs should do, and we had pleasant visions of the fine eating they would furnish later. But alas and alack, "the best-laid plans of mice and men gang aft a' gley."

The house in which we were living was very roughly and cheaply built and rats had bothered me greatly there. So I bought a small quantity of strychnine and sprinkled some over a piece of gingerbread, which I placed behind the stove, out of the children's reach. That day I had an Indian working for me, digging up some ground for a garden. I always had to have a garden, wherever I was. As the Indian sat on the back porch eating his dinner, I swept out the kitchen, inadvertently sweeping out the piece of gingerbread which I had already completely forgotten. As I saw it lying on the floor I stooped down and picked it up, thinking at first that I would give it to the Indian with the rest of his dinner. But it looked a little rough and "mussy," so I threw it carelessly into the swill-pail which I soon emptied into the trough in the pig pen. Then I went on serenely about my work.

In about half an hour, Captain Hamilton, an old bachelor sea captain who lived in another part of the house, came running to my back door, asking excitedly, "What in the world is the matter with your pigs? They act as though they had been poisoned!" Instantly, then, I remembered about the strychnine. Captain Hamilton and I rushed out to the pig pen, but when we reached there two of my precious pigs were dead and the other two seemed to be dying. For more than two hours we worked over those pigs, pouring warm mustard water down their throats and finally we saved them. But it was a prodigious job.

Afterwards, I frequently thought of what might have happened to me if I had given that gingerbread to the Indian instead of to the pigs. I fear I could not have convinced his tribe that it was an accident. The Coos Indians, so far as we knew, were gentle and friendly to the whites, but we could not expect them to stand for murder—and such it would have been if the native had eaten the poisoned ginger-bread. But "all's well that ends well," happily for me and mine.

In the early fall of 1854 I commenced teaching in Empire City. I was the first school teacher in Coos County. My husband was elected county school superintendent, also the first one in the county. In connection with his duties he had many amusing experiences, only one of which I will relate.

There was an old Missouri doctor in the village, a most excellent man, but whose knowledge of books and medicine was decidedly limited. But he had a wise, patriarchal appearance and inspired confidence with his patients generally. He had a considerable practice, naturally, as he was at that time the only person in the county who made any pretensions whatever to being a physician. Usually, this doctor's prescriptions were helpful, as he compounded them himself with drugs and medicines obtained largely from plants and shrubs found in his locality.

The good doctor had a daughter-in-law about twenty-six years old, and it occurred to him that teaching school would be a good occupation for her, especially as I now had a third little daughter and could not really spare the time for teaching. But I managed to get along with my family and my housework all right, and found my school teaching quite a relaxation. Accordingly, in a short time "Elizabeth" applied for a certificate. The old doctor and John Yoakam, both of whom were trustees, were present at the examination, which my husband conducted in his official capacity. The first question he asked was, "What is orthography?" The applicant squirmed and twisted and after some hesitation answered "I don't know. I never seed that teached!"

The next question was "What is grammar?" "Grammar, grammar," she repeated, wonderingly. "I don't know, I never learned grammar!"

The third question was "What is arithmetic?" Now Elizabeth was at home. Quickly she replied, triumphantly, "Why, that's to learn 'em to count!"

"Spell arithmetic," said my husband. But this was a puzzler. The poor girl stumbled over the long word, spelling it in half a dozen different ways, none of which was correct. After repeated trials the examiner discovered that her knowledge of "arithmetic" included only partial information regarding the first few multiplication tables. Elizabeth now grew sullen and silent, refusing to answer any more questions. Then the doctor brought the examination to a close, saying hopefully, in his broad Pike County dialect, "Wal, we-all knows 'Lizbeth knowed enough to learn the young 'uns all right, but I reckon 'cordin' to the law, she cain't get a 'stificate!" Thus ended my first and only rival in the school teaching field in Empire City.

I had all sorts of experiences in those early days, such as every pioneer woman must expect to have. Once a party of government surveyors came to the village and because of the unexpected roughness of the country they had been surveying, they found themselves almost in rags. They were anxious to find someone to make new outfits for them. Someone recommended me as a good seamstress, or as they put it, "a good hand with a needle." The men urged me to do their work and though I was busy enough with my three children, my housekeeping and my school teaching, I managed to make the entire lot of fourteen pairs of overalls and as many "jumpers." It was before the days of sewing machines and I had to do all the work by hand. Yet I made a suit a day, receiving one dollar for each jumper and each pair of overalls. That was big pay for those days, but I earned it all!

At this time my husband was in San Francisco on business and was detained there for some time. He sent us up by schooner a large box of apples and perhaps we did not appreciate them! They were the first apples we had seen since leaving the Umpqua Valley three years before. I know we did not waste a particle of those precious apples. They were far more precious to us than the famed golden apples of the Hesperides would have been. We reveled in apple pie and apple sauce, using the peelings and cores for jelly, which was truly delicious.

While I did not have a very high opinion of Indians in general, I did admire some of the handiwork of the patient, long-suffering squaws. They used to bring me berries of different kinds in fine, water-tight baskets, always woven in flexible style, with quite classical designs in them. Most of these baskets were made from the tender roots of the cedar trees and were strong and durable. Different kinds of grasses were also used for these baskets and frequently the squaws made excursions into the outlying forests to find exactly the kind of grasses they desired, for they must be strong and light and gathered at a certain stage of growth.

These industrious women also made a kind of matting that I thought especially lovely. It was of a delicate buff color, soft and closely woven with artistic native designs in contrasting colors. The squaws made their own vegetable dyes of various roots and grasses. I used a lot of this fine matting in those early days, but for many years now I have not seen a piece of it.

It was interesting to see the way the natives, both men and women, carried their burden baskets, as they were called. A large, loosely-woven basket, wide at the top and tapering to a point at the bottom, had a hand-woven band two inches or more in width, attached to it on both sides of the top. This broad band passed directly over the forehead of the burden bearer, who was usually a woman, with the basket itself hanging down the back. It was both astonishing and distressing to see the heavy loads the poor women often carried. Small wonder that they were bent and wrinkled while they were still young. Many of them had been really beautiful girls—that was evident. But most of their beauty had now departed.

> "Care and sorrow and childbirth pain,
> Left their traces on heart and brain."

Occasionally we would have a little scare about an Indian

uprising, and then for a time we would look with suspicion upon every native. As we lived somewhat beyond the most thickly settled part of the village, some of the Indians got into the habit of stopping at our house on their way to and from their *rancherie* to beg for a little bread and molasses, of which they were fond. Sometimes they would merely ask for a drink of water or anything else of which they happened to think. I can see now that it was merely curiosity that prompted their frequent calls. They wanted to learn all they could about the white people and their strange ways. Sometimes when my husband was away—and he was absent much of the time—some big black Indian, with a long dirk knife thrust into his belt, would stop at our house just as it was beginning to get dark. After peering around curiously he would ask in an apparently innocent manner, "Kah tilshel?" (Where is husband?).

I would be afraid to tell him the truth, so I would nod my head carelessly in the direction of the back yard and speak in an indifferent tone, although my "tum-tum" sometimes beat very rapidly, "Oh, mitlite kloshe illahee!" (around the place somewhere).

Then the old rascal would look at me with a queer, quizzical expression and drawl out in the remarkably scornful and skeptical tone peculiar to the Indian, "Wake mitlite tilshel! Nika nanich tilshel klatawa canim si——ah!" which interpreted into English means "There is no husband around the place. I saw him going far away in a canoe!"

Many and many a stormy night I was awakened by the rattling of the windows and doors and would sit up in bed shivering with fright, sure that the Indians were breaking into the house to rob and murder us. But we were never really molested. My two oldest little daughters were very fair children but when my third baby girl was born she resembled a regular Indian. She had long black hair, black eyes and unusually dark skin. On her left knee, the size of a quarter dollar, there was a dark-brown spot the color of an Indian's skin. This brown spot never disappeared. You may be sure I was thankful that it was not on her face! For several months I was really alarmed lest she should continue to resemble the natives and was actually ashamed to let strangers see her. However, she gradually outgrew the resemblance and in time became the handsomest one of the family.

For several years now the restless, murderous Rogue River Indians had been on the warpath, committing all sorts of dreadful atrocities, and the troops sent against them thus far had been unable to subdue them. They had finally affected the Coquille Indians so that they too could no longer be trusted and it was feared that these latter natives would in turn incite the Coos Bay Indians to hostility.

Because of these fears, it was deemed wise to prepare for emergencies and, accordingly, a fort was commenced at Empire City. A volunteer military company was organized and while some of the men proceeded to dig a deep trench on a sightly eminence near the center of the village, others cut or sawed down nearby trees of uniform size, stripped them of their branches and brought them to the location selected for the fort. The logs were then set down into the ground for several feet, the trench then filled with well-packed earth, the whole being thus formed into a strong stockade fourteen feet high and one hundred feet square. In the middle of the inclosed space a two-story block house, thirty feet square, was built of hewn logs. A guard house was also built and a strict guard was maintained day and night. The upper story of the block house projected five or six feet over the lower one and several "peep-holes" gave the inmates a commanding view of the adjacent country and made it possible for them to fire at an advancing foe from an elevation. This was considered a great advantage. This upper portion of the block house was ordinarily reserved for the women and children. It was reached by a ladder, which was drawn up after we were all inside, after the fashion of the ancient cliff-dwellers.

This pioneer fort was located almost on the identical spot

where the county court house later stood. For several weeks practically all the families in the settlement, and even those a distance from it, resorted nightly to the fort, fearing an Indian uprising in the dark. But finally confidence in the natives was restored. We believed ourselves safe and remained quietly in our homes. Our Indians never became hostile.

Perhaps one reason why they remained friendly during these trying times when neighboring tribes were pillaging and murdering was because our volunteer company made a pact or bargain with them.

There were five chiefs living with their little bands just below Empire City, around the places we now call "First Creek" and "Second Creek," and on down as far as Rocky Point. The natives always selected for their camps places where plenty of good fresh water could be found. This was an essential. The captain of our volunteer company, William H. Harris, held a big council with the Indians at Empire City. Our men asked the natives whether they wanted to fight or whether they wanted to be peaceable. The chiefs, all of whom were present at this council meeting, replied that they did not wish to fight, that their hearts were very soft and tender to the white men. But, they continued, if they did not wage war against the palefaces, the Rogue River and Coquille Indians would come in and kill them.

Our men told the Indians that they would protect them from these blood-thirsty neighbors if they would remain at their camps and notify the white captain whenever any strange natives came among them urging them to be wicked. Captain Harris also told them that if they would be the white men's friends, he would supply them with meat and flour indefinitely, so that they would never be hungry and need not hunt and fish all the time to keep alive. This last suggestion appealed strongly to the indolent Indian nature and it was immediately accepted by them. This bargain was kept inviolate on both sides.

Twice a week the quartermaster sent two men into the

woods for elk and deer and invariably they returned in a few hours with all the game their horses could carry. A mule pack-train was established between Empire City and the Umpqua, twenty miles up the beach, where there was a trading post or station of the Hudson's Bay Company where supplies were brought in regularly. Twice a week the Indians appeared at the fort for their rations, which were never withheld.

CHAPTER NINE

IN recent years considerable discussion has arisen concerning the origin or derivation of the word "Coos," the name of our own Oregon county. There are many different opinions regarding the origin of this name. All that I know personally about it is that it was called "Coos" long before we came and that was in 1853. I presume that after all at this late date, one person's opinion on the matter is about as good as another's. My husband always maintained that the name was derived from the fact that the cows of the Hudson's Bay Company at the Umpqua used to stray down into this Coos Bay area when grass became short and dry up there. This situation existed when there were green fields and meadows across the bay from Empire City. I remember such a time, even in my day. That was before the drifting sands, blown by the strong northwest winds, covered up the grassy meadows forever. Thus that locality became known as "Cowes Bay," as the lost animals were usually found there. My husband also declared, and many persons here agreed with him, that the natives were unable to pronounce the word "cows" as we do, calling it "coos."

I can readily understand how a name could be given to a locality in the manner just described, for Pony Slough or Pony Inlet, as we call it now, a short distance below North Bend, was so named by the Indians in early days because their ponies used to stray from Empire City to feast upon the luxuriant grass surrounding the slough. Frequently, some years later, when our own cows would be missing from their pasture at Empire City, my son or perhaps an Indian would search for them at Pony Slough. Here the animals were usually to be found grazing contentedly in the wide, grassy meadows.

Some have declared that the word "Coos" is of Indian origin, meaning "The Land of Pines." I think this theory has been adopted generally as being correct. However, I do not agree with those who accept this belief. In the state of New Hampshire there is a county named "Coos" but I have been told by persons familiar with that region that this word is pronounced in two syllables, "Co'-os," the accent being on the first syllable, usually.

Others again have stated that the word is of scriptural origin and point triumphantly to the sentence, "We came by a straight course to Coos," in the twenty-first chapter and first verse of the Acts of the Apostles, as proof of their assertion. According to many biblical students, this word is of classical origin and is pronounced, according to them, in two syllables, the same as that of New Hampshire, with accent on the first syllable.

On the early government maps the name of the bay and the river was variously spelled as Koos, Kowes, Kowan, Cowes and Cowan. "Kusan" seems to have been, and I think is still, the poetic or romantic name applied to the Coos tribe.

Rather recently a certain learned man, a philologist, has made an exhaustive study of the original Coos language. He says the name "Coos" is purely of native origin and is derived from the re-duplicated stem-word "Ku-kwis," meaning "south," which appears often in phrases like "Ku-semi-toito," (southwards). He also says the Coosas call their native language the "Hanis" tongue, which is now spoken by a very few persons, probably not more than a dozen in all, and will of course soon disappear entirely as a spoken language. There was also another ancient Indian language known as the "Miluk," which is now practically extinct.

The Chinook jargon was spoken by most of the Indians when the first white settlers came. I always realized then that the older natives knew and frequently spoke, especially among themselves, a language we could not understand. Sometimes I would ask them what they were saying but the squaws would only laugh in their foolish way and make no reply.

My own opinion regarding the origin of the word "Coos" is that the theory set forth by the learned man to whom I have referred may have some foundation in fact. This scholar has written a very scientific, technical treatise on the subject of the Coos language for the Bureau of American Ethnology, and who am I to question such authority?

In discussing this much-mooted matter with various natives and half-breeds, I have been told that the word "Coos" in their Indian tongue means "south" or "to the sea." This statement lends an additional element of accuracy to the opinion held by the savant. It suggests that the name itself was given to this section of the country originally by the natives in the interior, away from the coast. However, I might add in this connection that the Journal of Alex R. McLeod of the Hudson's Bay Company, whose party journeyed to the Umpqua River to recover the property of Jedediah S. Smith in 1828, which had been taken from him by the dastardly Umpquas, he refers to the natives of the Coos region as the "Cahoose" Indians. It may be that the early white settlers did not pronounce the name as the natives did. McLeod also refers to the "Shiquits River" as being in this vicinity. It seems natural for us to assume that by this he meant Ten Mile Creek, which empties into the ocean about ten miles up the beach from Empire City and which at times assumes the proportions of a small river. Judging from McLeod's account of the expedition, his party did not go farther south in recovering the stolen Smith property.

As you probably already know, this Jedediah S. Smith and his party were the first white men, so far as we know, ever to penetrate the Coos Bay country. Smith paused here briefly on his way north hunting and trapping, in 1828. His party was attacked by Indians at the Umpqua and most of them massacred. The story of Jedediah S. Smith and his adventures is a most interesting one. He was a colorful, picturesque and interesting figure of early days in pioneer fur activities.

I recall that sometime in 1854 a very serious and tragic occurrence transpired. As the circumstances were dramatic and unusual, I will relate them. One sunshiny day two young men, by name Burton and Venable, who had been prospecting for gold in this region, were traveling down the Coquille River in a canoe. They had at various times, had dealings with the natives and had experienced no trouble with them. As these two unsuspecting men paddled quietly along the placid river, two canoes, containing six Indians, suddenly shot out from the river bank and approached them. As they came nearer, the natives evinced every indication of friendliness. But as they reached the canoe of the white men, they suddenly seized and overturned it. As the unfortunate men struggled in the water, the Indians beat them mercilessly on the head with their paddles, soon killing them. Their bodies were then weighted down with stones and sunk in the river.

The Indians thought they had successfully covered all traces of their dastardly crime and believed that it would never be known. But in due time the bodies rose to the surface and were found by white men. The stream in which they were discovered was from this circumstance for many years known as "Dead Man's Slough," but this was a gruesome name and later it was changed to "Iowa Slough," by which name it has since been known.

Now it happened that a young Umpqua Indian, a mere boy, had been captured by the Coquilles some time before and had been cruelly tortured by them. This lad was devoted to a white boy by the name of Daniel Giles, a boy about his own age who had been kind to the unfortunate young Indian. This native lad was in the confidence of the Indians who discussed the subject of the murder of the two young white men freely in his presence. By using a little strategy he discovered who the six murderers were. Then he imparted his information to his young white friend and, acting upon this information, two of the criminals were found and promptly hanged by the enraged miners at Randolph.

One of the Indians was boastful and unrepentant to the last. He possessed the proverbial Indian stoicism. He admitted that he had killed the white men and declared that he was glad he had done so. He said he would kill all the white men if he could; that they had killed many of the Indians without cause and he wanted revenge. He said the white people were interlopers here; that they had no right to come into this country and take the red men's lands and turn the natives out. He was very eloquent. He said, "The Great Spirit sent the Indians here long ago to have all this land for their own. The elk, the deer, the fish, the fowl, all were for the Indian alone. The white man has no right to any of these things. He had his lands, his homes. The Indians did not disturb them. I have done the white people all the harm I could. If I had many men, I would do more. I am not afraid to die. I am a warrior and a warrior knows no fear. I die, but I go to the happy hunting grounds of my father and my father's fathers, and from there my spirit will urge the Indians to exterminate every white man that comes into this country."

Even at the last, this brave, proud spirit showed no fear. The other Indian was a coward and died like a whining dog.

Soon two more of the murderers were caught and hanged at Port Orford by a committee of outraged and angry white men. One other escaped and one still remained at large.

Not long after this several Indians came into Empire City. This was no unusual circumstance in itself, but it was noticed that some of their blankets bore in large letters, the initials of one of the slain travelers. As the natives could not read English, they were quite unconscious of this damning evidence. The Indian that carried the telltale blanket was arrested, tried by a jury, convicted, mainly on evidence furnished by the natives themselves, and sentenced to be hanged.

There was great excitement in the little settlement on the day appointed for the execution. Everybody felt that justice must be meted out and that the Indians must be taught a lesson, once and for all time. A novel gallows was arranged, made from a long, slender fir pole fixed into the crotch of a big wild cherry tree. My husband was "master of ceremonies" for this gruesome affair, and he told Pete, the guilty man, to confess his crime and "dirate wa-wa,"—that is, "tell the truth." He impressed upon Pete's mind that if he confessed and told the exact truth, he would go to the happy hunting grounds all right, but if he lied, "Sa-ha-le ty-ee hyas solleks." In English this means "God would be very angry with him."

Many Indians from the surrounding country were present at the execution time and all seemed deeply impressed by it, although they said little.

An amusing circumstance, though tragic in a measure, in connection with this dreadful affair was that in a day or two after the execution Indians in and around the settlement began hanging their dogs in exactly the same manner that Pete had been hanged. All over the *dancherie* hapless canines were seen suspended. We never learned why the natives thus sacrificed their pets, of which they were always very fond. Possibly they thought they were providing company for Pete on his long, distant journey, though they called him a "bad Injin" and professed to believe that he richly deserved his unhappy fate. The probabilities are that they had some superstitious idea that in killing their dogs in the same way that Pete had died, they were making a sacrifice that would bring them immunity from a similar fate. No amount of questioning by the white people could induce the Indians to reveal their motive in sacrificing their dogs.

We never had any further trouble with the natives of Coos Bay. And now I want to relate a story of a far different kind, one that has no such tragic ending as the one I have just told, although it did have somewhat tragic aspects. I have mentioned something about black sand mines and gold deposits and this story will be along these lines. It is both interesting and is also absolutely true—So I think it deserves a title all by itself. I will call it,

The Buried Treasure.

Following the discovery of gold in California in 1849, tales of the fabulous wealth to be found there naturally drifted to all parts of the country. Among the many persons that listened with absorbing interest to these alluring accounts were two young French-Canadian half-breeds, named Joe Groulois and Jean Baptiste. These men for some years had been living at the Hudson's Bay post at Fort Vancouver, hunting and trapping for the great company during the season. Upon hearing of the richness of the California mines they were eager to go and try their fortunes. Thus, early in the summer of 1851, they quietly saddled their fleet little Indian ponies and fared forth on their voyage of adventure and discovery.

Being experienced woodsmen, they had no difficulty in penetrating the wilderness, finally finding themselves among the Indian tribes on and near the Siuslaw River. Here they were most hospitably received by the natives, who felt honored at the presence of the two young and handsome half-breeds. Here the adventurous travelers remained for some time.

At last they decided to continue on their way south. Bidding their new-made friends adieu, they rode down the beach, pausing at the various Indian encampments on their route, and making friends of all with whom they came in contact.

In due time they passed Coos Bay, where they lingered for only a few days. Finally, they reached a little creek on the lower Coquille River where Joe Groulois stopped to get a drink of fresh, cold water. As he stooped down, he was attracted by the unusual golden color of the sand in the bottom of the shallow creek. Pausing, he thrust in his two hands and drew them forth full of the shining particles. Groulois had seen gold before. He had seen it mined in Canada, and he knew at once that he was not mistaken in supposing this yellow substance to be the precious metal for which they were journeying southward. He called his companion who came running at the excited, imperative tones of Groulois' usually calm voice, and Baptiste exclaimed in wonder when he saw the handfuls of glittering sand.

The golden deposit in the bed of the creek was undoubtedly a virgin one, never before worked, and probably never before perceived by man. Indians had been passing over it, or near it, for uncounted years, but they were ignorant of gold in any form and if they had seen this they were not interested in it. Of course, this extremely rich sand had not always been thus uncovered. Possibly some unusually high tide, or freshet, had washed away the gray sand and much of the black sand as well, thus leaving the golden harvest exposed.

The half-breeds immediately fell to discussing their best method of saving the gold they had discovered. It seemed useless to attempt this while the water of the swift little creek ran over it. Much of the fine gold would have been washed away as they shoveled it out, going down to join the sands of the restless sea.

They finally decided that the first thing for them to do was to divert the source of the stream almost entirely. Accordingly, they unpacked their short-handled shovels, which they always carried with them and tethered their ponies where they could graze farther up the stream on the lush green grass growing so abundantly there.

Both Groulois and Baptiste realized that they need seek no further for gold. No need to go to California when the sands of this northern land promised so abundant a harvest of riches.

The two half-breeds followed up the course of the creek until it was lost in the tangle of shrubs and the shadow of the woods, finding as they went along that the shining yellow sands were conspicuous throughout the entire course of the stream. Where the clear water issued from the ground, beside the trunks of mossy old trees, they started to turn its gentle course aside, digging another channel close beside the first, so that they might easily and quickly wash their shovelfuls of sand in it. When this new channel was at last finished, it was nearly dark and both Groulois and Baptiste were weary but happy in anticipation of the future. They ate their scanty supper of dried elk's meat, washing it down with black, unsweetened coffee boiled over a driftwood fire which they had made by rubbing two sticks together, Indian fashion, until they had caught a spark.

Early dawn saw both men up and stirring. After their hurried breakfast, which was but a repetition of their supper of the night before, they went at once to their pleasant task of gathering gold. Think of merely pushing a shovel down into the sand and drawing it up with a very considerable percentage of gold in it! This all sounds like a fairy tale, but it is really true.

I presume there are still many places in the world where this experience might be repeated even now, where there are virgin deposits of gold unseen and unsuspected that will eventually yield their hidden treasures to the keen vision of curious man.

The hardy, excited half-breeds scarcely paused to rest or to eat during that first eventful day. When evening came and they were obliged to quit working, both had quite a pile of gold dust to show for their strenuous labor. While they knew, in a general, somewhat unintelligent way, that they had stumbled upon an unusually rich deposit and that their discovery was important and would create some interest and excitement if it were known to the outside world, their narrow, ignorant minds could by no means grasp the full magnitude of it.

This was the place that afterwards became famous as "Whiskey Run." It has been estimated that over a million dollars' worth of gold dust was taken from this mine, first and last. Probably too, one-half of the gold was lost, being washed back into the sea, with the crude methods of working the sands. However, plenty of it was saved. One man said he saw a pint cup filled with gold dust from the work of three men for six hours.

Many of the miners of that day were indifferent about saving or taking care of their gold dust. "Easy come, easy go," is an old and true saying. Unless the miners had families or others dependent upon them or had some special object in view for which they needed money, they too frequently squandered it recklessly. As a rule, the miners were an honest lot, with a strict code of honor among themselves.

I have been told that after the Whiskey Run mines became more widely known, when the original discoverers had vanished and large numbers of men from all parts of the coast were working there, that sometimes a miner, after a successful run, would put several thousand dollars' worth of gold dust in his pockets and go down to Port Orford to enjoy a little taste of "high life." Here he would usually patronize the saloons liberally, "treating" his friends and their acquaintances frequently. It is also said it was not uncommon for him to remain about the place in an intoxicated condition for days, oblivious to the passing of time, and never being robbed of a single ounce of his yellow dust. Of course, gold dust was quite common—almost everybody had it, or could acquire it with a little exertion. Besides, it was rather cumbersome to carry.

The name "Whiskey Run" was bestowed upon this primitive mining camp because of the great quantity of whiskey consumed there. Brandy, whiskey and other liquors were usually considered an essential part of every miner's outfit in those early days.

You may be sure that the two half-breeds wasted no time in getting out the precious dust. They stayed closely at their posts. Occasionally, they were visited by Indians traveling up or down the coast. But these visitors were never curious and asked no questions. They had no conception of the value of the golden sands. Naturally, the half-breeds made no unnecessary explanations. The weeks flew by. The two men, working early and late through the long summer days, had by this time accumulated a large quantity of gold dust. This they had cached securely away, safe from the prying eyes of casual visitors. Still they had no adequate idea of the value of their holdings.

Late in the summer they learned from wandering Indians

that a large number of "Uncle Sam's Boston Men," as they termed the United States soldiers, had arrived at Port Orford, and that the little settlement there was lively and full of excitement.

By this time the half-breeds were wearying somewhat of their lonely work and naturally enough, yearned for some outside interest and diversion. They hesitated to leave their precious hoard alone fearing that some curious prowler might accidentally discover its whereabouts. Finally it was decided that Groulois, the older of the two, should make the first visit out and bring back to Baptiste a report of what was transpiring below. This course decided upon, Groulois mounted his pony and with a big bag of gold dust tied securely around his waist, under his red flannel shirt, rode merrily down the beach to Port Orford.

He was clever enough to conceal the possession of the gold dust from the soldiers he soon met there, but unfortunately for the lonely Groulois, he almost immediately fell in with a certain well-known Spanish woman, who had followed the troops from San Francisco. This handsome Spaniard, siren-like, employed her arts and charms on unsuspecting and unsophisticated Groulois to such an extent that his bag of gold dust soon passed from his possession to hers. The wily woman of course knew its value, and while showering smiles and favors on the unsuspicious half-breed, drew from him the whole story of the mines. She gave him a sack of flour, a side of bacon, some coffee and other necessities and advised him to return immediately and bring down to her all the gold dust he could possibly get. Then she would marry him, she said, and together they would sail far away to a wonderful country where they would be great "grandees" with their wealth. So she bade him hasten away to his treasure-house on the beach.

Poor, simple Groulois, simple only where an artful woman was concerned, readily believed all that this adventuress told him. He hurried back to his mine to slave day and night to secure sufficient gold dust to satisfy his ambitious lady-love. However, he discreetly refrained from telling Baptiste why he was so eager to take out more gold dust. He knew his partner would have scant patience with him in such a matter.

At last he had another big pile of the pretty, shiny stuff and once more he mounted his pony and rode merrily down the beach. The beauteous Spaniard received him with open arms, though it may be suspected that her ardor was caused more by the bag of gold dust carried by Groulois than by the appearance of the half-breed himself. Again she exerted all her wiles and at last succeeded in wresting from the amiable Groulois his entire supply of gold dust. Then, with smiles and promises of happiness to come, she outfitted him again with provisions and sent him back to bring her still more of the golden dust. Groulois unquestionably obeyed her and left Port Orford for his storehouse of wealth.

Hardly had he ridden out of sight before a coast steamer stopped briefly at Port Orford, and the treacherous Spanish woman, with her ill-gotten gains, embarked on it for green fields and pastures new. It was afterwards said that she had a troop of thirty or forty soldiers carrying the gold dust down to the steamer for her and that her holdings could not have been less than half a million dollars. This is probably a great exaggeration, but she must have had a very considerable sum, according to what Groulois himself told later.

Poor Groulois, happily unconscious of the impending blow, continued to amass more riches. When he felt that he had accumulated an amount sufficient to appease his beloved enchantress, though he had never entirely depleted his supply, he again wended his way to Port Orford. As his fleet-footed little pony trotted nimbly over the desolate sands, the half-breed's heart fairly sang for joy. Until his meeting with the divine Spanish woman he had never known what happiness meant. But now he knew! Visions of their rosy future together floated cloud-like in his mind, practical, hard-headed French-Canadian that he was.

Arriving at his destination in high spirits, eager to again

meet his inamorata, his rage and disappointment can perhaps be imagined when he learned that she had fled, taking his gold dust with her. But like many men of his race, he spoke few words. His emotions were too deep for utterance. He proceeded to fill himself with strong liquor, then exchanging some of his gold dust for a quantity of whiskey, he took his disconsolate way homeward.

Reaching the mine, he threw himself from his pony and his usually silent tongue now loosened by frequent potations, he told to the sympathetic ears of Jean Baptiste the whole tragic story of his disappointed love.

Together now they imbibed too frequently of the flowing bowl, endeavoring, as countless others have done before and since their time, to drown their sorrows. They succeeded in doing this to such an extent that in a few days they were wholly incapacitated for work, and in addition to this, they were becoming mentally unbalanced. But they still continued to drink heavily. They had no self-control left. It was impossible for them in their dazed condition to grasp the fact that they were unfitted for any sort of logical reasoning. At last, as liquor always does, it got the best of them. They began to imagine all kinds of dreadful things. They were really getting what is known in medical language as "delirium tremens." I have heard rough-spoken men term this the "Blue Devils."

The befuddled half-breeds now fancied that the white men from Port Orford were after them, chasing them, and trying to kill them for their precious gold dust. They hurriedly changed the hiding-place of their treasure, but even then they did not feel safe. Baptiste had a very large quantity of the dust, not having squandered any of his on beauteous Spanish women.

Finally, their agony became so acute that they could stand it no longer. They feared that their enemies, who were wholly imaginary, would never leave them in peace. They decided to depart from the place as speedily as possible. Accordingly, they hastily gathered up their store of glittering dust, putting it into one and two-pound powder cans, or buckskin bags, even placing some in small, closely-woven Indian baskets or pouches. Then they tied it all securely on their saddles with deer-skin sinews and dashed madly away towards Fort Vancouver. They fled wildly along, the voices and shouts of the pursuing white men ever sounding loudly in their ears. They feared they would soon be overtaken and murdered. They concluded to stop and bury their treasure, in this way escaping with their lives, at least.

They were traveling on a fairly well-beaten trail, probably the same one over which John Flanagan later established a pack-mule service from Empire City. They dismounted, tying their ponies to a near-by tree, and hurried off into the deep woods with their gold dust. They could not go far, however, as their burden was heavy and their fears great, and they were compelled to make several trips before their precious load was safe in the seclusion of the forest. At last they had their entire holdings in one spot. In haste and terror they frantically dug the earth away from the outspreading roots of a great cedar tree that sprawled not far from the trail, expecting every moment to feel the clutching hands of the remorseless white men around their throats. With trembling fingers they hastily deposited their yellow horde in the cavity they had excavated.

They marked the giant tree with signs and symbols they knew they could not fail to recognize later. They also took careful note of the entire surroundings. The roots of the great cedar turned and twisted in such an unusual manner as to set it apart from its fellows. By no possibility could they fail to locate this place again when their foes had left them in peace.

Although the wits of the half-breeds were dulled by drink, the instinct of the red man remained and they felt supremely positive they would have no difficulty whatever in regaining their buried wealth when they desired to do so. They covered their hiding-place with leaves, twigs and branches in such manner that the ground above and around it showed not the slightest trace of having been recently disturbed. The men felt that their secret was safe even from the prying eyes accustomed to reading the stories told in the woods by Old Mother Nature.

Very cautiously then they returned to the spot where they had left their ponies, and mounting them, hurried away, the exultant cries of their pursuers seeming nearer than before.

Hardly pausing to eat or sleep, ere long they reached the shelter of old Fort Vancouver, where they felt really safe at last. They were still in a serious condition from the great quantities of whiskey they had consumed and their breathless ride to safety, as they thought it. Their friends at the Fort immediately recognized the condition of the two men and set about restoring them to their normal mental and physical state. After a few weeks, when they were themselves again, both realized with considerable chagrin what the situation had really been.

Most gladly then would the half-breeds have returned to their secret hiding-place and to their gold mine on the southern coast. But the important season for trapping and hunting was at hand and they were required to go forth with the others and do their share towards getting furs and pelts for the company. Both Groulois and Baptiste were impatient and provoked at this unexpected delay in returning south and it was perhaps six months or more before they found it possible to ride down towards the place where they had concealed their treasure.

Miles before they reached that vicinity, they found to their consternation that a great forest fire had swept over the country since their flight from it. But they hoped, almost frantically, that the conflagration had burned itself out ere it reached their cache and surely the big cedar tree, with its unusual appearance, was still standing unharmed. In feverish haste, as may perhaps be imagined, they rode on. However, as they proceeded, they discovered to their horror, that the entire face of the country was changed. Desolate, brown wastes of land and blackened trees and stumps everywhere confronted their distracted gaze.

The disastrous fire that ravaged the lower Coquille at that early day is still spoken of with bated breath by surviving Indians and old settlers. It had obliterated every trace of their "witness tree" and all other landmarks with which they were familiar. The two half-breeds were fairly beside themselves with furious disappointment and despair. This then, was the pitiful end of their hard work, their hopes, their plans! It seemed too much to bear, even for men as stoical as themselves.

For weeks they searched with frenzied zeal for their buried treasure, but to no avail. The cache of gold still eluded them. Finally they gave up in despair and started to wash out more gold dust. But by this time others had heard of the rich sands and the French-Canadians had much competition. Besides, the values were giving out, as they frequently do in deposits of this character. The gray sands were beginning to cover up the valuable black sands.

Of course somebody will want to know if the half-breeds' cache of gold was ever found. So far as is known, it never was. Many have searched for it and doubtless many more will continue to do so, but always without success. For aught we know, it still remains in the spot where the frightened half-breeds buried it long ago.

Joe Groulois remained in that part of the country for many years, ever seeking his precious dust, and always being compelled to admit that he was baffled. It was difficult for him to relinquish the hope that some fortunate day he would find his lost treasure. I personally knew several men that sought for it from time to time, some of these with Groulois himself, but no one had any more success than another. Looking for it was like following a will-o'-the-wisp—it ever led them on, yet ever eluded them.

One of the young fellows that searched with Joe Groulois for the elusive treasure was Gus Bennett, a spirited Irish youth, my friend and neighbor, who loved adventure in any form. It was from Gus' own lips that I first heard the complete story of the buried treasure, which I have told here as he told it to me.

I believe there are some other versions of this story, but it must be remembered that a reliable person who knew Joe Groulois intimately, and who accompanied him several times in his search for his lost gold, was certainly in a position to give an accurate account of the whole affair.

Joe Groulois, naturally enough, loved to talk about this matter. However, he was usually silent concerning his acquaintance with the "Spanish woman." To Gus' friendly ears, Groulois repeatedly told the entire story, in detail, from the time he and Jean Baptiste left Fort Vancouver, bound for the California gold fields.

There is one vague rumor that floated about in connection with this buried treasure some years ago. It may be only a fairy tale, and probably is only that. But it is said that soon after the outbreak of the World War in Europe, two Germans came into the lower Coquille River country. These men appeared to be in poor financial circumstances. They kept much to themselves and asked few questions. Nobody paid any special attention to them. After spending a few days in the settlement, they purchased some supplies and provisions, together with a small camping outfit. Then they disappeared, apparently vanishing from the "haunts of men" for some time. Nobody knew or cared where they went. Months passed. Finally they re-appeared. They now seemed prosperous. But they did not remain long in the neighborhood. They drifted out of sight as mysteriously as they had come and were never again heard of in that locality. Some persons believe that these two strange men were German scientists of some sort, who had a method of divining where minerals were held in the ground.

There are other persons who honestly believe the gold dust has been found, not by the two Germans, but by others who have not announced the discovery.

The probability is, however, that the precious yellow dust

still lies where the trembling fingers of the terrified half-breeds deposited it in the depths of the forest. A new forest has practically grown up over that part of the country again. This makes it still more difficult to locate the place where the gold was buried. Possibly, a century or so from now, when this entire country has been denuded of all its timber, some fortunate man, industriously tilling his little farm, will unearth the buried treasure.

An interesting fact in connection with the great forest fire that destroyed the half-breeds' "witness" tree, as well as immense tracts of valuable virgin timber, is the story of the Indians concerning the origin, or cause of this most destructive conflagration. The natives claim, and they seem to have considerable evidence to prove their assertion, that a party of half-drunken white miners were visiting at the Indian camp on the lower Coquille River. These miners had brought with them a keg of whiskey from which they imbibed freely and frequently. In time, some of the miners became quarrelsome.

In one of their rowdy fracases, the keg of liquor was accidentally overturned, its contents spilling into the big camp-fire of the natives. This produced a spontaneous blaze which soon became uncontrolable. The fire spread with great rapidity, as forest fires usually do. Grass and twigs were dry and offered abundant fuel to the greedy flames. It was not long until much of the country was ablaze.

It is said that some of the Indians lost their lives in this dreadful holocaust. I personally heard of one Indian mother whose only child, a baby, was burned in its basket while the frantic mother, absent at the moment, was unable to out-distance the flames.

Gus Bennett also told me some interesting facts in connection with the quantity of platinum found in the early days in the old black sand mines near where Joe Groulois and Jean Baptiste worked so long a time.

This particular place was somewhat nearer to the old mining town of Randolph than the half-breeds' location, however. Although Gus was but eighteen or nineteen years old at this time, he was deeply interested in everything pertaining to mining. It fascinated him, as it has done many men older than he. During the years of his residence on the lower Coquille, he had spent considerable time washing out gold from the beaches and creeks near his home. He really took out a lot of gold, first and last, though his methods of course were the same crude ones employed by most miners of that day. Even today I cannot really say that any better or more profitable method for saving the gold has been developed.

A miner would take a shovelful of the rich black sand, in which he could see very plainly the tiny particules of shining gold. He would immerse the shovel in water and "wash" it, or "rock" it gently back and forth. The sand gradually washed away, leaving the fine gold, which was heavier than the sand, deposited in particles or rings around the sides of the shovel, or in the bottom of it. Of course a man had to be expert to save much of the gold. You will readily see too, that much of the fine gold dust must have been lost by this process.

There were several other methods and ways of saving the gold, or at least, attempting to save it. Some miners used blankets, the fine flakes of richness being caught and held on the soft wool nap. Still others employed skins of animals, the hair side uppermost, of course, to catch the gold.

Gus said that he and those working with him in the black sand mines were greatly impeded in separating the gold by the presence of a certain white substance that occurred in profusion and which constantly covered their apparatus, even though they occasionally ceased operations and removed the offending deposit. The little lake into which they ran off their "tailings" was white with this annoying substance. There seemed no way in which they could overcome it, as it was present in ever-recurring quantities. They knew, in a wholly disinterested way, that this troublesome stuff was called "platinum," but that meant nothing to them. They were mining for gold, not for trash!

Finally someone suggested that perhaps this platinum might possess some value. Acting upon this suggestion, Gus wrote to a well-known assaying firm in the city of New York, describing the substance as best he could and its abundance in the sands. He ended by telling the firm he understood it was called "platinum." He inquired what it was worth and what the firm would pay for it. In due time an answer came. The firm assured him that the substance was undoubtedly platinum. They offered fifty cents an ounce for it, but Gus would have to pay the postage or express charges out of that! Naturally enough. Gus did not accept the offer. The matter of the platinum really seemed too small and worthless to bother him. Now, with platinum found in but few places in the world and its value very great, this story, while absolutely true in every detail, sounds ridiculous. But time changes many things!

Colonel John Lane, son of General Jo Lane, the first territorial governor of Oregon, was one of many men interested in early days in the black sand mines near Randolph. His brother, Simon Lane, owned and operated the Pioneer Mine there. One day Colonel Lane came along with a large glass pickle-jar in his hand, this jar being one of the old-fashioned square-sided bottles, holding a quart or more. Seeing Gus standing idly near, the Colonel asked Gus to hold the jar under the spout of the sluice-box while he caught some of that "shiny stuff" to send to his little niece, Jennie Lane, in Portland. The genial Colonel remarked that he thought the glittering, silvery substance would please her childish fancy. Gus did as the Colonel requested, and in a few moments the jar was filled to overflowing with the "shiny stuff." This little incident gives one some idea of the abundance of platinum there at that time.*

*An interesting sequel to the incidents of the glass pickle-jar that was filled with platinum in a few minutes in the year 1880, was found in an item that appeared in a prominent Portland, Oregon, daily newspaper of 1925 or thereabouts. This item stated that the old Simon

Lane house in Portland had been sold. In the general clearance made necessary by the change in ownership, there was found in the basement of the house an old-fashioned glass jar, or bottle, filled with some sort of a silvery substance. Upon being assayed, the contents of the jar proved to be largely platinum, worth about $2350.00.

It is improbable that much platinum is in those black sands now, though assayists say it is still found there. However, it would not be so easy to get now as it was in those distant early days. One old miner, a very reliable man, told me some years ago that he and his wife took out one-third of the world's supply of platinum from a mine near them during the World War. They used only crude methods, too.

The tailings Gus mentioned have been worked over and most of the values extracted and the drifting sands of the sea have covered most of the deposits. But perhaps hidden far below the surface, there can still be found large deposits of platinum and gold, which will richly repay the man who finds a way of getting them out profitably.

Gus Bennett also told me an interesting tale of his experiences near the same old Whiskey Run district where Grolois and Baptiste worked so long ago. He said that he and several others investigated the sands near there and found them very rich in gold and platinum. These valuable sands were not so far below the surface as to make working them impracticable or too difficult. These boys marked their location plainly, then went home to prepare their mining equipment, intending to return as soon as this was ready. Not long after they had left the place, a violent storm arose, such as we often have on the Oregon coast. After the storm had spent its force, Gus and his partners went expectantly to their location. But to their disappointment and dismay, they discovered that the storm had piled huge drift logs over it, and to remove these so as to reach the rich sands beneath, would have been a Herculean task. Doubtless these rich sands still remain there to this day. Perhaps other storms have taken out the driftwood. Who knows?

CHAPTER TEN

AFTER coming back from North Bend, which really had no name whatever at that time, we lived in Empire City for about six years.

Life there was not very interesting or exciting for my husband as there was really nothing for him to do in that small community. With his restless, adventurous spirit, such an idle existence was decidedly monotonous for him, and for some time he had been urging me to consent to move over to the Coquille Valley, where fine farming and timber land could be taken up under the Donation Claim Act. By this time, a number of settlers, with their families, had taken claims on the river and were industriously hewing out homes in the heavy forests of fir, cedar, maple and myrtle.

Both the latter two are hardwood and the myrtle is an especially beautiful wood, susceptible of a very high polish. It is found in only a few places of the world, one of these being in the Holy Land. Oregon myrtle is only just now beginning to be appreciated for its beauty and rarity. In early pioneer days, the settlers cut down their groves of fine myrtles, to clear the land for agricultural purposes. All these magnificent old trees were burned to get the bottom lands under cultivation. Today these lands would be worth much more with the myrtle still standing than they are cleared.

Finally, after much deliberation on my part, and persuasion on the part of my husband, I consented to his taking up a donation claim of three hundred and twenty acres on the Coquille River. The place he selected ·was considered an unusually fine one, consisting of about half bottom land, the rest being heavily timbered. I had been teaching school nearly all the time we had been living in Empire City and I dreaded giving up this rather congenial occupation for the hard, unending grind of a pioneer farmer's wife in a region where the natives had been known to be hostile, and where privations would necessarily be many.

Perhaps what influenced me more than anything else to consent to this last move was the fact that late in May, 1859, a colony of about thirty persons from the city of Baltimore, Maryland, under the leadership of Dr. Henry Hermann, arrived in the Coquille Valley to make their permanent homes. Dr. Hermann was a physician of good standing in the big eastern city from which he had come. Constant practice of his profession there had undermined his health, and it became imperative that he should seek an entire change of climate. Like many other thoughtful men of that day, his mind turned to the far west. He made a long trip to California, including southern Oregon, in his itinerary.

He was so pleased with the resources, climate and potentialities of what is now Coos County, that upon his return to Baltimore for his family, he lost no time in organizing a colony of his friends and acquaintances to accompany him to this new, faraway country. His prophetic vision already saw this wild, distant land settled, civilized and developed into a great future.

The men in Dr. Hermann's company represented various trades and professions. It was planned to meet the requirements of a pioneer country. Among the men were house and ship carpenters, shoemakers, cigar makers, cabinet makers, one locksmith, several farmers, one piano maker, some blacksmiths, some miners, one tinsmith, one music teacher and one physician, Dr. Hermann himself. Thus equipped, they expected not only to supply all their own needs, but those of the other settlers along the Coquille as well.

Most of the men in the Hermann colony brought their families with them, some of the children being mere babies in arms while others were fully grown. The emigrants came by way of the Isthmus of Panama, and had a long and varied experience before reaching the end of their journey. After arriving here, some of the members of the colony became dissatisfied with the prospects for speedy settlement and civilization in this new country. They were keen enough to realize that it would require practically a lifetime of hard labor to clear off the dense forests and build comfortable homes in such a heavily-wooded wilderness. Accordingly, these persons returned to California, where they could even then enjoy some of the comforts of life without such a long, unequal struggle against the forces of nature in the north. Personally, I always admired these people who came to this decision early instead of remaining in this densely wooded region, with its heavy, depressing rainfall.

The Hermann colony brought the first piano to Coos County. It was a big, square instrument of that day and weighed a prodigious amount. It was a grand piano, though! It was probably far superior to most pianos made today, for in that early time most of the workmen on these instruments had learned their trade, or profession, in Germany, where skill was a necessity in the business. The piano was unloaded from a ship at San Francisco after having made the voyage around Cape Horn from Baltimore. Then, after a considerable delay, it was transferred to a small schooner sailing for Coos Bay. Then ensued a long, stormy voyage up the coast, which was none too good for this remarkable instrument. The schooner reached Empire City, where the pioneer piano was unloaded with much difficulty. Here its most complicated adventures really began. How to get this huge instrument over to the Coquille River, which seemed very far away then, was the perplexing problem. But "where there's a will, there's a way."

At last, after much planning and much hard labor as well, the piano was placed across or over the gunwales of two large canoes, which were then towed up to the head of what we now know as "Isthmus Slough" by a big row-boat at a time when a strong, incoming tide was running. Reaching the Isthmus without mishap, fortunately, the piano and canoes were with immense difficulty transported over the two intervening miles of portage between there and Beaver

Slough, through which the instrument must be taken before reaching the Coquille River.

Beaver Slough, at that time, had a mass of tangled vines and shrubs reaching almost completely across its entire surface. This, together with the frequency of beaver dams that had to be destroyed before a passage could be gained, made the journey through its dark waters anything but easy or rapid. But it was certainly an interesting and novel experience for those hardy pioneers who were bringing a little of their far eastern culture to this land of cultural darkness. Before the much-traveled piano was safely out of the slough, one of the canoes ran upon a snag, tipped dangerously, and despite frantic efforts to prevent such a catastrophe, the piano slipped into the dark waters. However, after almost superhuman efforts, lasting for hours, it was recovered and eventually arrived at its destination in the home of Mr. Henry Schroeder, a most delightful gentleman.

Now the piano was dried out and thoroughly cleaned by Mr. Schroeder, who was a master craftsman at this delicate work, and apparently the grand instrument was as good as new, despite its many misadventures.

Mr. Schroeder had a large family of charming young people, all of whom were musically inclined, and for many years his hospitable home was the center of joyous festivities. The sturdy pioneer piano lent its notes of sweetness and harmany to innumerable dances and scenes of merriment.

Practically all of the German immigrants were fond of music and dancing and many of them had a good knowledge of music as well. Unfortunately, this historic instrument was burned in a fire that destroyed Mr. Schroeder's home in 1889. Looking back upon the bygone years, it seems to me that this piano was actually worth all the effort and expense it cost, for it undoubtedly helped to make a primitive environment a little brighter and pleasanter for many.

At the same time that the piano arrived at Empire City, there also came a portable sawmill with a big boiler and engine, two huge burrs for a flour mill, and a complete blacksmithing outfit. By the time all these articles had been transported to their final destination on the Coquille River, they had cost their owners about sixty dollars a measured ton, that is, from Baltimore.

The Hermann colony had also purchased and shipped a small stock of general merchandise, expecting to trade with and supply settlers, but these goods were lost when the old brig *Cyclops* was wrecked on the Coos Bay bar. The only articles the colony saved were a plough and a couple of saws, but I presume they were thankful to have even these.

The Indians had been engaged to carry the goods of the newcomers over the portage between the Isthmus and Beaver Slough, and how to get all these terribly heavy articles over puzzled them for awhile. They were never very quick at solving such problems. However, they finally evolved the plan of cutting down strong, slender young trees, or saplings, peeling the bark from them, laying them on the ground, and then sliding the piano and other extremely heavy articles over their smooth surface. Most of the actual work was done by the squaws, who carried immense loads on their backs, bending almost double in the operation. The braves considered it beneath their dignity to do any actual manual labor. They stood back and gave short, curt orders that the poor women unhesitatingly obeyed.

It always rather amused me to see an Indian and his squaw in a canoe together. He would sit serenely in the most comfortable place in the clumsy craft, while she stood and did the paddling, under his orders, for her dignfied lord and master.

In all my experience with Indians, I never saw or knew of but one instance where the husband showed any regard or consideration for his wife. The exception was "Ticky Tom," who used to bring me those wonderfully-dressed and inexpensive wild ducks and geese about which I have already spoken. Many, many years later I visited Tom and his good little wife, Kate, at their cabin in the sandhills down the bay. They were in need, and I had brought them some sup-

plies of fresh meat and other food. Poor old Tom lay upon
his bed of suffering, mumbling incoherent words I could not
fully understand. But the general tone of his sentences was
something about Kate, who sat beside him, at frequent intervals patting his hands lovingly and murmuring words of
comfort and endearment. The time came when we had to
leave, and as I stood beside good old Tom, he looked up at
me pathetically, saying over and over again, "Take care of
Kate, take care of Kate! Pretty soon I go away, take care of
Kate!"

But I must hark back to the coming of the Hermann colony. In my reminiscences of poor old Tom and his wife,
I was almost forgetting the newcomers in their extremity.

After many trials and tribulations, their belongings were
at last safely carried through Beaver Slough, but just before
reaching their destination, one of the boats capsized, and
Dr. Hermann's valuable library, together with his surgical
instruments, sorely needed in this new country, and many
other treasured articles went to the bottom of the river.

Some of these things were not recovered until the following late summer, when the water in the stream was low, and
many were never recovered. It seemed a cruel and unjust
blow that things they had cared enough about to bring clear
across a continent at great expense and inconvenience, should
be lost or ruined in this manner, when so near their journey's
end. But such is often the fate of pioneers.

For a great many years, Dr. Hermann was the only
physician in a radius of probably sixty miles. Every pioneer
doctor naturally has many unusual and interesting experiences, as he is always the recipient of his patients' confi-
dences. It is to the faithful family physician alone that the
"family skeleton," if there is one, is bared, and in this wild,
remote and romantic part of the world Dr. Hermann must
have listened to many remarkable death-bed confessions and
revelations. In those early days there were many strange
characters hereabouts, many that had known happier days,
and many that had histories they would not have liked the

world to know. This distant bit of the universe was a good place in which a man could hide and try to forget his past, if he desired to forget it.

Dr. Hermann kept his secrets well. His experiences with both men and wild animals, his many narrow escapes from death in various forms, on land and on water, all combined to make his pioneer life interesting and unusual. If he ever regretted having left his comfortable eastern home for the rude cabin in the vast forests of southern Oregon, I never heard him admit it. I do not believe he did regret the change. Although his life was filled with far different matters than those to which he had been accustomed, there were compensations too. For one thing, he recovered his health. It is a pity that he never found time or opportunity to compile his reminiscences into book form. They would have made highly interesting reading. Dr. Hermann was a well educated man, and quite a linguist. He had been a student at one of the big German universities where he later became a professor of anatomy and surgery. There had been plenty of adventure and romance in his life there. He had taken a somewhat active part in the revolution of 1838. After the defeat of the patriots, he came to America, where he could enjoy the social and political liberty denied him in his native land. The coming of the Hermann colony was undoubtedly a great factor in the development of the Coquille Valley. People like myself, for instance, who had hesitated to take up claims over there because of its isolation, hesitated no longer. We thought, and apparently with good reason, that if so large a party of intelligent persons from old-settled eastern communities could see sufficient attraction there to induce them to leave home, friends and advanced civilization, and cast their "lives, their fortunes and their sacred honor" here in this remote wilderness, there must be something worth while in it, after all. Apparently distance from the scene was needed to give one the right perspective.

It was in October, 1859, that we moved over to the Coquille. We went by small boat, really just a frail skiff, up the bay to the Isthmus, to which point my husband had already transported our meager household belongings. From the Isthmus we all walked over the rough, narrow trail to Beaver Slough, where a flat-bottomed, odd-looking small boat was kept for occasional travelers. Beaver Slough was an exceedingly tortuous stream about five miles long, flowing into the Coquille River.

It may be recalled that I have told about the time that Mrs. Dean and my little family were the first white women to make the trip through that locally-historic waterway. That memorable little voyage occurred the first day of April, 1854. Going through Beaver Slough then was certainly a unique experience—one that will in all probability never again be known.

With the advent of the railroad and the consequent disuse of the stream as a medium of travel and commerce, it has become filled with brush, logs and vegetable matter. Now it is practically only a damp, marshy jungle filled with the malodorous but medicinally valuable "skunk-cabbage." The great yellow flowers of this plant give an almost fantastic appearance to the ancient stream that played so important a part in our local pioneer history.

I think most persons would have thoroughly enjoyed this little journey down Beaver Slough, had they taken it a few years after I did, when they would have felt certain that no actual danger was involved. But it really seemed a perilous undertaking then, even to a pioneer woman, to ride through this remarkably unusual and picturesque inlet. In many places the stream was very deep. Every few rods it turned and twisted abruptly. Trees of spruce, alder, fir, cedar, tasselwood, wild cherry, crabapple, willow and various other kinds, with many large shrubs, lined the banks. Many of these were intertwined with wild blackberry and other vines that formed an almost impenetrable tangle. In many places the brush and branches reached far over the stream, sometimes threatening to push us out of the boat if we relaxed our vigilance.

At that time neither my husband nor I could swim, and with three young children and some household goods in our little craft, we had need of caution. But what made this short voyage interesting and most unusual was the fact that it was the home of countless busy beavers, from whose presence the stream had been named. The beaver is surely the most industrious animal imaginable. My husband was obliged to paddle up to the bank every few hundred feet, sometimes oftener, disembark and destroy the ingenious dams the animals had constructed, across the narrow stream. We knew, however, that only a short time would elapse before the obstructions would be rebuilt, and that a traveler coming through the slough the next day would probably find as many dams there as we had found. One of the most interesting things about these remarkable little creatures is the way they construct their dams, not only as regards its architecture—if I may use that word—but the methods they employ in their building operations. They build their homes, or lodges, as they are sometimes called, under the water, so that no enemy can reach them. The fox is one of their bitterest foes, but even he, with all his cunning, can not touch them when they are protected by several feet of water. Sometimes, however, the water is not sufficiently deep to afford them the protection they desire, so these clever little builders proceed to increase the depth. They go up on the bank of the stream where they decided to locate, or where they have already located, and select some tree, sapling or shrub that seems suitable for their purpose. Then they gnaw around this with their sharp teeth until it is entirely cut through. Usually, most trees growing near the water lean towards it, and when they are felled, they naturally fall into the water. The shrewd beavers take advantage of this fact, which saves them a vast amount of labor and time, though they never seem to grow weary or discouraged, even when their toilsome work is being constantly destroyed by officious prowlers, both human and otherwise. Some naturalists claim that only one family of beavers cut on a tree at a time, but I do not know whether or not that is true.

If the tree is too long for the place where the beavers intend to put it, they proceed to cut it into proper lengths. Old trappers have told me that the space around a beaver's lodge looks like a wood-chopper's pile. Most of the pieces are cut about three feet long. This appears to be about the size the animals can handle most readily. After the tree is finally in the water, the beavers push it along with their paws until it is in the desired position. Then they bring mud, sticks and small stones in their forepaws to weight down the branches or saplings, until they sink to the bottom. They continue in this manner until they often have quite a formidable barrier across the stream. This was the case in Beaver Slough. I think my husband must have destroyed at least eighteen or twenty dams while we were going over that five miles of Slough.

The beaver is distinguished by a broad, flat tail, the meat of which used to be considered quite a delicacy. I never cared for it, however, as it seemed to have a kind of slippery, slimy taste, if you can imagine what I mean by that. One other peculiarity of this wonderful little animal is the fact that his hind feet are webbed, while his fore feet are not. Thus he is equally at home in the water or on the land. Some clever person has said that the beavers are the first engineers, and we must believe this when we see the almost unbelievable way in which they engineer the construction of their abodes.

In later years I have gone through Beaver Slough when no attempt whatever was made to row a boat through it, because of the numerous beaver dams encountered. Instead, a man walked along a towpath, with a rope, dragging the boat behind him. Whenever he came to another annoying beaver dam, the air would be filled with choice profanity until the whole atmosphere seemed positively blue, to the great amusement of the occupants of the boat, who considered this one of the most picturesque features of the trip.

I fear there are not many of these ingenious little creatures left in this part of the country. I know there are none in the Beaver Slough district. There may be a few colonies of them in some of the remoter streams that civilization has not yet reached, but in all of our navigable waterways hereabouts, the industrious beaver is practically extinct. The beautiful glossy brown fur of these marvelous animals was coveted by many and trappers hunted them mercilessly.

After many hours of slow paddling, pausing often to annihilate another beaver dam, we finally emerged into the Coquille River, a beautiful stream, the banks of which were lined with great forests coming down almost to the water's edge. Many of the old maple and myrtles, patriarchs of the groves, leaned far over the brink, almost touching some of those on the other side, and forming in places a lovely green avenue, with the blue river flowing underneath. As we emerged from the slough into the river, my husband exchanged the paddle for oars, as the stream was broad and smooth here.

At last we reached our new home, a small, two-roomed log cabin, situated in a clearing among grand old myrtle trees. This was truly a glorious spot, if one cared for solitude and nature's charms only. Our nearest neighbors were more than a mile away, and like ourselves, were true pioneers, having literally hewn their log house from the virgin woods, as my husband had done.

In a short time I made our tiny cabin look quite homelike, with a big, rough fireplace and plenty of hardwood logs to burn. I also began having regular hours for my little girls to study and recite their lessons. There was no school and no prospect of one, and I could not bear the thought of my children growing up in ignorance of books and all that books imply.

Soon we purchased some cattle, pigs and chickens, and almost before we realized it, we had our own little farm. My husband gradually cleared off more land and after our first two years on the Coquille we had a fine vegetable garden, as the soil was naturally rich and only needed a little cultivation to make it very productive.

About this time a man named Bottolph came into the Valley and started a small nursery. This Mr. Bottolph was an interesting man and I am sure you would have enjoyed knowing him, especially if you had been isolated as we were. He had a keen wit, into which a sting might occasionally creep. We thoroughly enjoyed him. He brought in a little breath of the outside world that was extremely refreshing to us, after our long absence from older centers of life and activity. He was a civil engineer by profession and it was he who surveyed and platted the town of Myrtle Point, as the place where we then lived was afterwards named.

Among Mr. Bottolph's other accomplishments, he had a very musical voice and often entertained us with his songs. I well remember that he was the first person I ever heard sing "Ben Bolt," that pathetic ballad that Du Maurier many years later made famous in his book, "Trilby." Bottolph's keen sense of humor helped him over many rough places, for in a new country such as that one always finds plenty of "rough" spots. He was a frequent visitor at our little cabin and always a welcome one. He was both alone and lonely.

He enjoyed reading our books and magazines, warming himself at our huge fire while smoking and "swapping yarns" with my husband, who was also a great story-teller. I recall that one evening as he was leaving, he asked if I would lend him a candle, as his own supply was completely exhausted. As I handed the candle to him I inquired if he would not like a second one, also. "Oh, no," he replied instantly, with a sly twinkle in his eye. "That will be plenty. If one candle will last your big family until bedtime, it will surely last me until morning!"

In 1860— I think that was the year—Bottolph was elected county surveyor, beating his opponent by only four votes. In the course of time he received official notice to come to Empire City, the county seat, to qualify for the office. It was quite amusing to hear him describe his experiences on this occasion. He had the usual delays and difficulties in going through Beaver Slough and as there was neither a boat or a canoe at the Isthmus he concluded to attempt walking to Empire City, about thirty miles away. The trail was the flimsiest pretext possible for a road; the hills were steep and brushy, making the entire trip very slow and difficult.

When he reached the county seat, it was raining and almost dark. He was cold, wet and very hungry. He had never seen the metropolis of Coos County before and he was greatly disappointed in its appearance. He confided to me later that the place consisted of a few shacks and about thirty people! After considerable scouting around he found someone that gave him a hot supper. Then he started out to find the county clerk, the official before whom he was to appear. Finally he succeeded in locating this worthy personage in a shack designated as the "Court House," but he was busily engaged in an absorbing game of poker. He listened to Bottolph's story of why he was there; then he leaned back in his chair, looked at him a moment, and then requested Bottolph to wait until the game was finished, when he would attend to the official business. Naturally, Bottolph could not refuse this request. At the conclusion of the game, at which the clerk was the loser, the important business was taken up and concluded with dispatch. Mr. Bottolph always enjoyed relating this story, for it seemed so typically western to him as to be unique.

In December, following our arrival on the Coquille, my fourth little daughter was born. Her first cradle was made from a champagne basket that Mr. Bottolph gave me. My husband put rockers on it and I made a little mattress for it of soft white down plucked from the wild ducks' breasts. In this primitive bed my wee maid slept as soundly and sweetly as any royal princess.

Christmas came when my baby was just two weeks old. My other children called her "Mother's Christmas present." Our holiday perhaps could not be called a "merry" one, but the children enjoyed it and my husband and I enjoyed seeing them happy. My baby kept me rather busy about that time, but old Santa Claus is a thoughtful fellow and had arranged for some presents for my little people long before. We had no Christmas tree in the house, but we had hundreds of them all about us in the beautiful out-of-doors. The children hung their long, knitted stockings around the fireplace and seemed to be perfectly satisfied with what they found on the following morning.

It was interesting to hear them calling back and forth to each other in the dark, early hours of Christmas Day and delightful to their elders to watch their happy faces, illuminated by the blazing logs in the fireplace, as they examined their treasures.

Some may wonder what my children discovered in their stockings. I assure you that they contained little that would satisfy the ordinary child of today. The children of fifty or more years ago were more easily pleased. They were not so critical or sophisticated as the little folk of this generation. They were not spoiled with too many expensive toys and other valuable gifts. My little people found candy, of course, bright-colored sticks of peppermint, cinnamon and wintergreen, suspiciously like some that the "Twin Sisters" had sold weeks before. They also found lumps of white sugar and big pieces of molasses taffy that tasted exactly as though it were home-made. They found several kinds of cookies, too, though there was not a bakery in hundreds of miles. Naturally, as my family consisted entirely of girls, each stocking contained a doll, though I must admit that those for the younger children, aged five and seven, were merely "rag" babies, with painted cheeks and eyes made of black beads. However, my girlies were not in the least critical and adored these dollies as much as though they had been the latest Parisian creations. Each stocking held new shoes, with bright copper tips, and best of all, each found in her stocking enough lovely all-wool brown merino to make a warm winter dress. Of course, each one found a book, as they were omniverous little readers, and good old Santa had obligingly sent the very volumes that each wanted most.

Oh, yes, I had almost forgotten to say that each stocking contained a handful of hazelnuts in the very tip of the toe. The youngsters were inclined to feel slightly aggrieved at this gift, as hazelnuts were very plentiful about our cabin. But this disappointment did not trouble them long and, take it all in all, they were a thoroughly well-satisfied and happy little family.

My husband and I were extremely fond of reading and subscribed to several newspapers and magazines, but frequently we were annoyed and disappointed because there was much delay in getting our mail. Some of it we lost entirely. On every letter we received we paid twenty-five cents postage. I think we paid that on the magazines too. Once we were without any mail for six or seven weeks, which seemed like a year to us, and then we were rewarded with a big armful.

I recall how my husband and I would sit down before our big fire after the children were asleep to read and enjoy our belated mail, and how we did enjoy it! While we were engrossed in reading the old news of the outside world, from which we were so entirely separated, we would completely forget ourselves and our surroundings. Sometimes we would rouse with a start to find the narrow walls of our little cabin encroaching upon us.

Of course we had no regular mail carrier. Whenever anyone went to Empire City, forty or more miles away, which was the only post office in the county, he took with him a large, clean sack, in which to bring back the mail for practically everybody on the river. The trip to and from Empire City consumed from four to five days, that is, if one happened to strike the tides right. If he found them unfavorable the trip might require a week.

The manner of distributing the mail was necessarily very primitive: the settlers that received it last usually being the losers. At the first stopping-place that the amateur mail carrier reached, the entire sack of mail was dumped out on the table or the floor, the settler taking therefrom his own mail which the postmaster had obligingly put in one package. Of course some attempt was made to distribute the mail according to the location of the various settlers, but this was difficult and often impossible to do successfully. Usually one settler would remove from the sack the mail belonging to his nearest neighbor, if the carrier was not going in that direction, which was often the case.

At every place where the carrier stopped, invariably the entire contents of the sack were thoroughly investigated, for everybody was not only eager to claim all that was his, but he was also curious to know what the other settlers were getting. With these frequent handlings, much of it being hurriedly and carelessly done, the natural result was that papers and magazines often went astray. Much of our mail showed plainly that it had been read and re-read. This has no reference to letters, which were always kept inviolate. But other mail was sometimes regarded as public property. This was done with no intention to be dishonest, but merely a desire to become acquainted with what was happening outside, especially among his neighbors!

By this time we had added another room to our "abode," as our family was a little larger. I papered the walls of our little home with newspapers, using the New York *Tribune* for this purpose. In this way we all learned Longfellow's "Hiawatha," which was first published in the *Tribune.*

"East Lynne" came out in the Cincinnati *Weekly Times* about 1861 or thereabouts, and I can truthfully say that our papers were in demand all over the river. I knew this pathetic story almost by heart, as I also used some of the *Times* in my wall-papering activities.

> "Great Caesar dead and turned to clay,
>   Might stop a hole to keep the wind away,"

you know!

About this time "Bleak House," "Dombey and Son" and

"Little Dorrit" all by Charles Dickens, were published for the first time in America by *Harper's Monthly*. Naturally, I was completely absorbed in these fascinating novels and always waited most impatiently for the next installment to arrive. But often I was disappointed in the belated arrival of some of the numbers and a few I never received. Evidently other people enjoyed the stories too! Once a certain settler told me, in the frankest manner possible, that he always felt "terrible disappointed" when he failed to get our magazines to read. He added that he hoped we did not mind his taking them out for awhile!

In these later years I have often thought of what a perfect sportsman's paradise the entire Coquille country must have been in those early days. But the whole region surrounding us was the same then. It fairly teemed with game. We were rarely without some kind of delicious wild meat. When my husband was absent, the neighbors kindly shared some of their abundance with us. Every family in which there was a man or a half-grown boy, usually had more game than they could use. It is undoubtedly a fact that without the game, fish, shell-fish and berries provided by kindly nature, the pioneers would occasionally have found themselves in sorry straits.

I recall one day shortly after moving to the Coquille country, I chanced to glance towards our pasture and saw, to my delighted surprise, an immense elk grazing there. He was truly a magnificent specimen and appeared to feel entirely at home. Every few minutes he would lift his splendid head, would seem to listen attentively for a brief period, then he would complacently resume his munching of the short green grass. The sun shone on his glossy flanks and they glistened like rich brown satin. I quietly sent the two oldest children over to the nearest neighbors, about a half mile away, asking him to bring his gun and shoot the elk for us. But his wife sent back word that her husband had already killed three elk that day and was then gone with the horse and sled to bring in the carcasses.

After our unusual visitor had disported himself in our pasture for several hours, he suddenly disappeared. I was actually glad that we had been unable to slaughter him. It seemed positively inhuman to sacrifice such a glorious creature unless we were really in need of fresh meat, which we were not. Soon after the disappearance of the elk, I happened to look in the opposite direction and saw a big black bear trotting off as fast as his short legs would carry him.

We never concerned ourselves greatly about black bears, although we never cultivated their acquaintance, particularly. They were said never to attack a person unless first provoked into doing so, and you may imagine that we never made any attempt to provoke them! They were fierce and terrible fighters when aroused and some of the earliest settlers in the Valley had been unfortunate enough to have dreadful encounters with enraged bears, especially mothers with young cubs. Occasionally a bear would steal a pig from our pen and then my husband would set a simple home-made trap and catch Mr. Bruin. Some people professed to like bear meat, but it never had any attraction for me, although I occasionally fried or broiled some of the steaks. I have been told that a bear killed after the black huckleberry season—they were especially fond of these berries—furnished some of the finest, sweetest and best-flavored meat in the world, the flesh at that time resembling that of the choicest ham.

Speaking of bears reminds me of a little experience we once had that might not have terminated as happily as it did. One day the children and I were out in the woods picking black huckleberries, with which the country abounded. While we were busily engaged at our pleasant task, one of the children cried out, "Oh, mother, see that funny big black dog, eating berries!" I looked in the direction she indicated and to my consternation saw a gigantic black bear standing up on his hind legs eating energetically from the berry bushes. I called out loudly, and as he heard my voice he dropped to the ground, turned and looked at me for an instant, and then hurried off into the woods as fast as he could go.

Somehow berry picking had lost its zest for me that day, and I hastily gathered my little brood about me and started for home, looking anxiously at every clump of trees we passed. As the entire country was heavily wooded, and also well watered, thus providing secure shelter for animals, it was naturally full of predatory beasts, in addition to those of gentler nature. Settlers were few and far between and these fierce denizens of the wilds had things pretty much their own way most of the time.

The mountain lion, or the cougar, as many call him now, was probably the most ferocious and desperate animal of them all, just as he remains today. He was always a creature to be dreaded, both by man and beast, as he gave absolutely no quarter. He was such a stealthy, sneaking brute that it was sometimes difficult to protect oneself against him. He rarely came out in the open to fight, but skulked in the shadows and sprang out unexpectedly upon his quarry. It was estimated that one panther alone killed at least forty deer in a single year. Even the lordly elk was not immune from attack by this vicious beast. Bands of elk and deer, numbering from fifty to two hundred were often seen by hunters and settlers, and they said that wherever such a company of these beautiful, harmless creatures went, the long, tawny form of at least one panther lurked near, waiting for a favorable opportunity to pounce upon an unsuspecting victim.

I remember a case where a man living on the lower river was attacked by a panther as he was walking along a lonely trail in the dusk of the evening. The brute had evidently followed him for some distance, biding his time, and waiting for a secluded spot in which to attack. Finally, he sprang upon the traveler's back just as he reached a particularly dark place in the forest. The attack was so unexpected and the onslaught so vicious that as the man felt the great beast lunge upon him, burying its claws in his back and neck, he thought for a moment that his last hour had come. But with the true pioneer's instinct for self-preservation, he almost intuitively reached for the bowie-knife in his belt. Drawing it out, he slashed as best he could at the creature clinging tenaciously to him. Fortunately, the man's arms were clear and he was able to inflict some injury upon his assailant. The maddened brute screamed in rage and pain, and seizing the man's rather long hair in its powerful grasp, literally tore a portion of the man's scalp from his head. Then he sprang to the ground and bounded away into the forest. Luckily, the poor man was not far distant from a settler's cabin, and finally he succeeded in reaching it, more dead than alive. However, he was young and strong and eventually recovered from his terrible experience, though when I saw him some months later, he still wore a sort of cap over his head, to cover up the frightful wound and the loss of his hair.

I also recall that probably twenty years or more after this occurrence, when we thought the country was becoming quite civilized and fairly free from panthers in the vicinity of a settlement, a young girl of my acquaintance, Charlotte Nicholls by name, was attacked by a panther as she was riding into Empire City one dark night. Charlotte lived on South Slough, about four miles from Empire City, where she often visited friends and relatives. She was a fine and fearless horsewoman. On the occasion of which I speak, she was accompanied by her brother, who was also on horseback. That night they both rode spirited animals, fortunately. They were traveling on what is still known as "The Cammann Wagon Road." This was an especially heavily wooded part of the country, with great black forests on either side of the road, and no light save that of the distant stars to guide them. Even a lantern could not have availed much in that inky darkness, though it might possibly have saved them from attack by a panther, as these brutes fear a light or a fire. But the near proximity of the tall, black trees would prevent a light from casting its gleam very far, surrounded as they were by these ancient woods.

Suddenly as Charlotte rode fearlessly through the black night, a prowling panther sprang upon her horse's back. Charlotte, being perfectly at home on a horse's back, did not lose her head. Both she and her mount comprehended instantly what had happened. With a frightened squeal the horse gave a great leap forward, fortunately thus throwing the panther's hold free, but as the beast fell he raked the horse's sides with his sharp claws, leaving raw, bleeding welts there.

You may be sure that the horse had the bit after that, and when a half hour later they raced into Empire City, both he and his rider were almost exhausted. But plucky Charlotte did not indulge in tears or hysterics. She only declared vehemently that if it were daylight, and she had a good "varmint" dog and a gun, she would take a fresh mount, start out for that panther's scalp, and not return until she got it.

The entire Coquille Valley was a "real" sportsman's paradise in those days, and as I have told several true stories concerning my young friend Gus Bennett, and his experiences, I think you may find another one or two of Gus' tales interesting.

Gus had the true hunter's instinct. He loved this sport. It had been bred in his bones through generations of sporting ancestors in England and Ireland. While Gus lived on the lower Coquille with his father, he had a close friend, a boy about his own age, named Bill Perkins. They frequently went out on short hunting expeditions near their homes. One late summer, about the year 1877, when Gus was perhaps nineteen years of age, he and Bill decided to go out on a "big" elk hunt. The boys had two objects in view in making this trip. I suppose that the principal one, in reality, was to have a glorious time together, roughing it and camping out in the wilds in true pioneer fashion, masters of their own destiny. Their secondary object was to provide sufficient elk meat to last their respective families throughout the winter months.

They both had spacious but primitive smoke-houses and made a yearly practice of curing their winter and spring supply of elk meat, deer meat and pork, while the animals were in prime condition. These two boys lived on the lower Coquille just about where the river joins the ocean. Their sole

companion on this epochal hunting trip was Gus' dog, a very
sagacious and well-trained dog. He had been Gus' "pal"
on many previous trips into the forests and glades. The first
night out, the boys camped near the headwaters of Bear
Creek, as it was even then known. Gus declares that they
were probably the first white men that ever had been in that
locality, though the early Volunteer Company from Empire
City had sent their hunters into the lower Bear Creek region
as they passed through, to provide fresh meat for the men.
There was never any difficulty about having plenty of game
in that neighborhood. The boys located a suitable place in
which to camp for the night, found a big pitch-wood stump
near by and soon had a royal fire burning.

For a few minutes they sat and watched its cheerful blaze,
discussing future probable events of their expedition and
wondering what sort of "luck" they would have on this particular trip. To be out camping in the wilderness entirely
alone, entirely on their "own," was a new and thrilling experience for them. Before this, they had always accompanied
older men who assumed the responsibility of the entire affair. But the boys thought it was grand to be alone.

Presently Bill picked up a bucket and started down to the
bottom to dig a hole in the soft, moist earth to get some
water for drinking and for their coffee. He left his gun, an
old muzzle-loading rifle that his father had brought across
the plains in 1850, leaning against a near-by tree. As Gus
still sat silently before the fire, his thoughts wandering afar,
the gun in easy reach of his hand, he suddenly heard a noisy
rustling in the young fir trees close by, followed by a loud
"woof." Looking up quickly, he was amazed to see an immense elk, confronting him, with slightly lowered head. He
was not more than fifteen feet away. Though the boy's
pulses leaped excitedly, he did not lose his presence of mind.
It was but the work of an instant to seize Bill's old gun, aim
and fire at the beautiful intruder. Without uttering a sound,
the great creature fell dead in his tracks.

Bill, hearing the shot, ran hastily up from his task below, asking anxiously, "Gus, what were you shooting it?"

"Come and see," answered Gus, briefly.

Soon both youngsters were bending over the body of the prostrate elk. Naturally, they were jubilant. This was a wholly unexpected prize. A monarch of the forest had practically thrown himself at their feet!

This circumstance shows the great abundance of game in that locality in those days. A little later the boys gathered boughs of fragrant fir, piled them into heaps and lay down upon them. They had no blankets or other coverings. They needed nothing more than some of the fir branches laid over them as the night was warm and balmy. After discussing their plans for the morrow, they fell asleep. Blessed with perfect health, they slept soundly. Several hours later, as Gus, in the wonderful Land of Dreams, was battling for his life among a band of hostile savages, he was awakened by feeling his dog's cold muzzle rubbed over his face. Full of sleep, the boy spoke roughly to the animal, bidding him be still. In a few minutes the dog returned, but again Gus ordered him to be quiet. But the faithful creature still persisted, this time pawing the ground vigorously, leaping up to Gus' side and by many signs endeavoring to make his master understand that something unusual was happening. During all these attempts to arouse Gus, the sagacious dog had uttered no sound—not even a little whine had come from him. But now, after the dog's third attempt to get attention, both boys arose, and following the eager dog, found a big black bear greedily devouring the carcass of the elk, which the boys had left where it fell.

Instantly, Bill snatched his gun, while Gus seized a flaming torch from the pitch-wood log and held it behind Bill's shoulder, so that he might take accurate aim at Bruin, who had fled to the refuge of a near-by tree. Bill fired, and the bear came tumbling down, boys, bear and dog for a brief moment being apparently indiscriminately mixed in the unexpected scrimmage, which was soon terminated by the bear

making off into the deep woods. Boys and dog followed for
a short distance, but it was still dark and the chaparral bushes
and other small trees made it impossible for them to see far
ahead.

The next morning, however, they found the dead body
of the bear near the scene of conflict. Of course the boys were
highly elated over this second victory, gained with scarcely
an effort on their part. Still, they were true hunters and did
not wholly relish the thought of having their game come to
them, asking to be shot. They preferred to experience some
of the thrills and excitement of actual hunting. The other
way seemed too much like taking advantage of helpless and
unsuspecting creatures.

At early daybreak the following morning the lads were up
and stirring, ready to make a good long day of it. They were
hungry and eager for their breakfast. They partially skinned
the elk, cut some thick slices from one of the hind quarters
and skewered them on sharp sticks of alder wood. Then they
inserted the opposite end of the stick firmly in the ground
close by the blazing coals. They turned the sticks from time
to time as the meat cooked, finally having it done to their
taste. Gus said this was food fit for the gods, and I do not
doubt that he was absolutely right. The elk steaks were
washed down with black coffee and home-made bread they
had brought with them. Then the boys were ready to start
forth on their adventure. Long before the lads had risen, as
they lay on their forest couches ere the day broke, talking
quietly of their plans, they had heard a peculiar and wholly
new sound that had immediately attracted their attention.
Gradually, it dawned upon their consciousness that it was the
trampling of many feet, or hoofs, upon the ridge above them.

These boys, accustomed as they were to the ways of wood
folk, rightly conjectured that it was a large band of elk,
traveling from one part of the country to another. And such
it proved to be. The animals were emigrating from Curry
County, adjoining Coos, where settlers were encroaching too
closely on their ancient domains. The youngsters were full

of eager excitement at the prospect of soon encountering a big band of elk. Cautiously, their guns in hand, they crept up the side of the steep hill.

Reaching the top of the ridge at last, they saw there a narrow road, or trail, not more than three feet wide at its broadest part, worn and cut deep with innumerable hoofs, as though a vast herd of cattle had passed over it. Along the sides of this road, many of the slender fir and cedar trees showed torn and broken limbs, where the antlers of the elk had brushed them in their crowded passing. A heavy fog hung over the landscape, obscuring all but near objects. Upon reaching the road Bill, with the true hunter's instinct, had dropped to his knees in a listening attitude, partly hidden by the drooping branches of a large tree. Suddenly he emitted a low whistle, and Gus, looking in the direction indicated by Bill's pointing finger, saw a huge elk standing about fifteen feet away, looming terribly big in the fog. Almost immediately Bill took aim and fired, the smoke from the old muzzle-loader, combined with the fog, completely enveloping the scene for a few minutes. When it finally cleared away, the elk was seen to be standing in apparently the same position.

Now it was Gus' shot. He sighted carefully and fired, the air again being darkened by the smoke and fog. When the haze had lifted, the boys were again surprised to see what appeared to be the same elk still standing in the same place. Gus was about to fire again when Bill whispered excitedly, "It's my turn now," firing as he spoke. Anxiously the boys waited for the smoke to clear away. At last it vanished sufficiently for them to see that the elk was gone. Then cautiously both boys stepped forward. Guns in hand, they advanced slowly, looking cautiously on each side, fearful of finding a wounded and enraged elk, but they saw nothing. Unhindered, they pressed still farther forward, soon reaching a place in the road where a giant fir tree, with outspreading roots, had been torn from the ground, probably in some fierce winter gale. In the deep hole thus formed, the boys found, to their utter amazement, three elk, two dead and one wounded!

Each shot of theirs had gone home, each claiming a separate victim. The poor wounded elk was soon put out of his misery and after taking all the meat they desired from the carcasses, the boys cached it securely from prowling beasts and went on their way over the ridge, following the wide trail made by the elk.

The lads could scarcely contain themselves, so excited and eager were they to actually see the entire band together. They had not proceeded far when rounding a bend in the road, they came in sight of a great, brake-covered glade, where an immense herd of elk was grazing. The fog had lifted and the air was clear. The wind blew fresh against the boys and no hint or scent of their presence was wafted to the glorious creatures beyond. Quietly the youngsters crouched behind a sheltering stump and deliberately counted the number of elk before them. Three hundred and sixty! Three hundred and sixty full-grown elk sporting in the morning sun, full of lusty life and vigor, beautiful, wild and majestic! It was wonderful, a magnificent sight, one that the boys could never forget.

Occasionally some of the graceful creatures would lift their heads, apparently sniffing the breeze to learn of any lurking enemy. Gus said it seemed at these times as though a small forest of branching limbs had suddenly grown up before their eyes. I greatly doubt if a larger band of elk was ever seen together before or since in the history of this county, though I have heard old settlers say they had seen bands of elk numbering a thousand or more. However, I fancy they had not actually counted the animals, as the boys had done, and one is apt to be deceived, especially when the animals are moving or milling about.

These elk that the lads were fortunate enough to see undoubtedly constituted one entire herd that had emigrated in a body to new pastures. They had without doubt exhausted their supply of feed in their former home. Instinct told them where fresh feed might be found.

Several days later, as the boys were returning by a somewhat different route from the one they had taken in starting out, they paused briefly at the cabin of an old settler who spoke of the immense band of elk that had recently passed his place. He declared that it was like a herd of buffalo seen in crossing the plains. He said he thought there must have been at least a thousand in the band, and was surprised when the boys told him they had counted this same band and gave him the exact number it contained. On the homeward trip the lads came unexpectedly upon an old cow elk standing in the brake with her two big babies beside her. She was decidedly in fighting mood, as elk-mothers usually are when they have little ones, and the boys beat a hasty retreat. They could have killed her, easily, but that would have meant starvation for her calves. Gus said that this little trip netted his family and Bill's all the elk meat they could use for the entire winter, and if they had so desired, they would have had no difficulty in getting enough to last them a year or more. But they really never needed to lay in a big stock ahead, as the supply was always unlimited.

Gus was full of interesting incidents of his own experiences both on the lower Coquille and in the high mountains. We have several times spoken of the panther and his stealthy, sneaking, remorseless ways of attack. The story that Gus told me about this brute is very thrilling. At one time Gus' father was expecting some very important letters in the mail, which arrived at Randolph only once a week, and he asked Gus to ride over to the post office and get them. Now, horseback riding was always fun for Gus and he enjoyed going after the mail. The few miles' trip furnished a bit of entertainment and diversion from his usual dull routine. Exciting news sometimes came with the mail carrier, who arrived any time when the tide allowed him to make headway with his rowboat.

Upon this particular occasion of which I speak, the mail

man was very late, not reaching Randolph until nearly dark. Gus received the expected communications, lingered to have a friendly little chat with the carrier about life on the upper river and the outside world in general, and it was fully dark when he finally prepared to start for home, seven miles away. As the settler at whose place he had left his horse saw him saddling up, preparatory to leaving, he remarked, quietly, "Gus, I think you had better stay here tonight. There's a panther up there on the hill and I don't like the way he acts. I don't usually take water from these critters, but tonight I did. He seemed, somehow, to have the best of me. I think he is after a calf. You stay here tonight and we'll get him in the morning!"

But young Gus had no fear of these "varmints." Besides, his father was anxiously awaiting his letters.

"I think I'll ride on," he replied. "I'm not afraid of the fellow. I've met panthers before and they've usually run away before I could get a shot at them. I'll fix this one if he bothers me. Good-night!"

Gus mounted his horse and started out. The road, or trail, lay for some distance up a very steep hill, where Gus was obliged to hang practically on the horse's neck to keep from falling off his back. As he reached the top of this hill, the horse breathing rather rapidly, Gus suddenly saw through the darkness two gleaming balls of fire confronting him, at the same time hearing the angry snarl of a panther. Instinctively, Gus reached for his pistol, intending to end Mr. Panther's career abruptly. To his horror and consternation, Gus discovered that he did not have the weapon with him. Then he remembered what he had done. As the pistol was somewhat heavy and awkward to wear when not necessary, he had removed it from his belt, placed it on the table at the settlement and then had stupidly forgotten all about it. As the pony saw the beast before him, he snorted furiously, backed down the hill a few feet and finally turned complenty around. Then Gus, to his further horror and amazement, saw another pair of glaring eyes, belonging to the mate of the panther ahead.

The horse was frantic, Gus helpless. Suddenly, the panther in front bounded up on the low-hanging limb of a near-by tree, and the horse, in a frenzy of fear, dashed madly forward. The trail was like all trails in that part of the country at that time—narrow and tortuous, with stumps, limbs and roots of trees often protruding over it. Gus could ride it like a madman in the daytime, but in the inky darkness, it was a totally different proposition. He could not afford to take any chances with a couple of earnest panthers following closely behind him, so he gave the horse his head, and lay flat on the saddle, the upper part of his body resting on the horse's neck, while the terrified creature fled wildly through the dark forest.

The poor horse was grass-fed and incapable of long continued exertion or effort. Every few minutes he would pause to rest, his breath coming in great gasps. He would pick up his ears and appear to be listening for a brief spell, then, as the soft pat-pat-patter of the panthers' coming behind him was heard, he would dart away again, to repeat the same performance in another few minutes. Imagine Gus' emotions, if you can! He did not know how long his horse could continue this running game and he did not enjoy the prospect of a single-handed, unarmed battle with the two persistent and cruel creatures that were following him. Finally, after five or six miles of this torturing experience, they reached the rail fence of Gus' own domain. The patter of the panthers' footfalls was now no longer heard. They had evidently gone off on the scent of some new quarry, probably a defenseless deer. But Gus had no quarrel with the brutes on that account. He was thankful to have escaped merely with a wild night ride and a perilous chase. But the panthers secured some victims that night, after all.

The next morning Gus counted twenty-four big, fat dead wethers that were to have been delivered to the butcher the following week. However, Mr. and Mrs. Panther paid dearly for their awful night's work. That evening Gus' unerring rifle got one of the guilty animals, and a few days later he shot the other.

But to get back to my own adventures.

There were many coyotes, wildcats and coons that were extremely troublesome in those early days and they sometimes made midnight visits to prey upon the settlers' livestock or poultry, though they never attempted to attack people. I had raised a number of fine chickens, and for some time I had been annoyed by having coons come at night to kill my precious fowls. They had also helped themselves generously to my growing corn—another bad habit of theirs. I finally grew tired of providing free meals for these sagacious little thieves and determined upon drastic moves to rid myself of their unwelcome attentions. Accordingly, I selected an old, sick hen, killed her and sprinkled her liberally with strychnine which seemed to be my favorite media for committing such murders.

After preparing the fowl, I left it in a spot where I knew the inquisitive little coons could not fail to find it. Early the following morning I made the rounds of the place, and to my great satisfaction I found eight dead coons—three in the garden and five outside of the fence. That seemed to me a pretty good night's killing. As a result of this wholesale slaughter, I lost no more chickens for some time, though I had to repeat the remedy occasionally.

CHAPTER ELEVEN

WE never went hungry while we lived on the Coquille, although sometimes our larder was not very abundantly supplied. I believe that the earliest settlers there—those that came in 1854 or 1855—did suffer some privations. Usually they got their provisions from either the Umpqua or the Willamette Valleys. Sometimes three weeks or more would be required for this trip, if the streams were swollen or if there was snow in the interior.

The settlers brought their supplies in by pack-mules, and generally, they purchased a full six-months' supply, if they had sufficient money to do this. Sometimes everything at home would be exhausted before the "gude mon" returned from his long, hard trip. Occasionally before starting out for their season's supply some of the men would go over to "Johnson's Diggings" or down to the beach to some of the black sand deposits and "wash" out enough gold dust to pay for their goods. It sounds like an easy way to get money, but it was rather a slow process. Perhaps not many persons nowadays would be satisfied to make a living in such a tedious manner. But in those early days, these mines were a real bonanza for the settlers, as there was little opportunity to earn money unless one had a trade he could use. But opportunities for using any trade were extremely limited.

My husband used to go farther afield for his prospecting, often going as far away as Idaho, which was then, as now, considered a very rich region for gold. He sometimes brought home quite a lot of the precious metal, most of this being in the form of nuggets. I have a ring now that was made from a nugget he found in Idaho. I prize this ring highly. But we did not depend wholly upon mining or prospecting for our sustenance.

After the first two months on the Coquille, we had plenty of fresh butter, milk and eggs. In summer I pickled enough butter to last us through the winter. Fresh fruit, such as apples, pears, peaches and plums, was extremely scarce and seldom in good condition. None of the orchards on the river had yet come into full bearing. Everything in the nature of fresh fruit of which I have spoken was brought either by irregular boat from San Francisco or packed over rough mountain trails from the interior. Such journeys usually spelled disaster for perishable fruits. We could occasionally buy dried apples, not of good quality, however, at twenty or twenty-five cents a pound. Fortunately, there was in season a great abundance of delicious wild fruit, about the same varieties we had at Empire City.

The wild fruit on the Coquille was really far superior to that on the bay in size and flavor, doubtless due to the greater warmth of the valley climate. In addition to the wild fruits of the Bay region, we had on the Coquille quantities of black raspberries, or blackcaps, as they are now generally called. We were all fond of these delicious berries and I dried bags of them and also wild blackberries every year for winter use. These berries when dried seemed to contain all the flavor and sweetness that pure air and warm sunshine could bestow. I made quantities of jelly and preserves, too, from these wild fruits, as the children loved them and I considered it wise to give them some sweets. Wild crab-apples, gooseberries, currants, grapes, elderberries—the blue variety only—we never used the red ones, as they were said to be poisonous, and blackberries all made especially fine jelly.

Wild cherries also grew abundantly, but we never used them, as some persons said they too were poisonous. Salal berries were extremely plentiful everywhere, as they are now, and they certainly did look inviting and beautiful in their long, full clusters of rich, dark fruit. Although they looked so fine, the white people never seemed to make any use of them. The Indians prized them highly, not only as food, but also as medicine.

In those days we had no air-tight cans or glass jars, though many of the former were used in the big eastern cities. I used to dry corn, beans and peas in considerable quantities, and

they helped greatly in solving the problem of providing a
variety of vegetables in the winter. Carrots, parsnips, cab-
bage and a few other things frequently remained in the
ground the entire season. We had a primitive little smoke-
house and in this we cured all the bacon and ham we needed.
This was delicious, too, and in my opinion, far excelled in
flavor all the high-priced products of modern methods and
days. We also smoked and dried a lot of elk and deer meat
and if you have ever tasted these you will not need to be
told how good it was. I still had to make my own tallow
candles, and I continued to make them for many years thereafter. I also continued to make soap, usually of the soft variety, though occasionally I made some that was hard, for
bathing use.

We had no carpets, but many home-made rugs and some
beautiful skins of bear and panther for floor coverings, with
numerous elk and deer skins as well. Then I had a lot of
the lovely soft matting that the squaws wove so skilfully.
But I did not value this as much then as I did my fine skins.
I had wonderful feather beds and pillows made from feathers that we had plucked from the wild fowl that were so
plentiful in this region. In season, we enjoyed innumerable
wild ducks and geese, both of these being food fit for a king.
I endeavored to make the best of everything we had. I think
I must have been a very good manager in those days. It was
a case of necessity, I presume. But if I was a good manager,
I really deserve no credit for it, for that quality must have
been inherited from my thrifty Holland-Dutch ancestors.

By the time we had been living on the river for a year
or two, a good many other settlers had arrived and naturally
this stimulated frequent rural gatherings and amusements.
There was a fine comradeship among them and they assisted
each other in every way possible. Of course everything was
exceedingly primitive and crude, but we expected that.
Whenever a new settler came into the valley, located his donation claim, cleared a small patch of ground and had selected and cut the logs for his new habitation, he would notify

his neighbors that he was ready for their assistance. Then
the good people would come from far and near, bringing
their families with them. While the men "notched, rolled
and fitted" the logs, the women cooked, quilted or merely
visited. At noon there would be a big feast with all the good
things it was possible to obtain.

The pioneer women in that locality were noted for being
most excellent cooks. Thus, throughout the entire day the
work and the play continued. When the friendly neighbors
finally departed for their respective homes that evening,
they had the satisfaction of knowing that they had left the
stranger in their midst the framework of a substantial log
house or cabin. The work of the day was known as a "house-
raising" or "log rolling." Everybody thoroughly enjoyed
these occasions, for they not only meant that another family
had settled in the valley, but that once more all hands had
gathered together for a jolly, sociable time.

There was, of course, the ubiquitous "quilting-bee" for
the women, the men coming in for supper and the day usually ending with an old-fashioned dance. Most of the pioneers
were very fond of dancing. They were nearly all young
people and thoroughly enjoyed the amusements of youth.
However, dancing was by no means confined to the young.
The oldest among the pioneers found quite as much enjoyment in tripping "the light fantastic" of that day as the
younger generation did. As my husband was absent most of
the time while we lived on the Coquille—he was prospecting
in Idaho and elsewhere—it was difficult for me to attend
many of the neighborhood festivities. This was, after all,
not a great sacrifice for me, as I was not particularly fond of
dancing. My four children and my little farm, which was
not so little, after all, kept me more than busy.

The pioneers, entirely dependent upon their own resources for amusement, lost no opportunity for gathering
together. On the Fourth of July, 1859, a big celebration was
planned at Meyersville, afterward known as "Ott," and
now for more than half a century "Myrtle Point." Great

preparations were made to observe the occasion fittingly. Deep trenches were dug in the ground for preparing barbecued meats, roasting potatoes and cooking peas or any other vegetables obtained at that time. A sheep was to be roasted whole, also some pigs. One of the promoters of the celebration was a German, who was deeply interested in the success of the affair. He was speaking to me about the number of cakes that would be required for the occasion and I protested that he was providing too many. But he stoutly declared that "Many beobles will be there—lots of beobles—dree or four hundred beobles at the very leastest!"

As the happy result proved, the man was entirely right in his calculations. The celebration was a huge success, not an accident marring the pleasure of the day. Binger Hermann, then a youth of eighteen years, and later a popular congressman from our state, delivered the oration, and did it very well, too. The year previous my husband delivered the oration and young Binger Hermann had read the Declaration of Independence.

After the exercises and the fine barbecue dinner were finished, most of the young people, and many an older one as well, commenced dancing about three o'clock in the afternoon. They continued this fascinating amusement without interruption until after daylight the next morning. People generally arranged matters at home so that they might spend two days in celebrating—if they so desired—which they usually did. Most of the floors in the neighborhood were what was known as "puncheon" floors, and were not conducive to graceful or even very comfortable dancing. However, little attention was paid to such a slight annoyance.

Probably few persons nowadays know what a "puncheon" floor really was. I think it was a strictly pioneer affair, and one that was in general use in a wooded country. I believe I mentioned earlier about sleeping on a floor of this kind our first night at Empire City. A "puncheon" floor is one that is made of split logs or else logs that have been hewed down and smoothed off as much as possible. This work was always done by hand in those early days and of course there were many inequalities in a floor of this kind.

The music for these pioneer dances was always furnished by a "fiddle," as the violin was usually designated. Occasionally a dance was held at Mr. Schroeder's hospitable home and then the tones of the historic piano were mingled with those of the violin, or perhaps several violins, as some of the Hermann colony were masters of that instrument. It seems as though all rural neighborhoods have always contained at least one person that could play the violin, and he was always in demand for their rustic dances.

Speaking of the violin, reminds me that at one time, even no longer than seventy years ago, many persons considered the violin an unholy instrument—a device of King Pluto himself. I well remember the excitement that was created in our little Baptist church in Fairfield over this matter of the violin. A broad-minded, up-to-date member of the congregation had visited New York City and while there had attended religious services where the violin had been a special feature. Upon his return home, this traveler suggested the same innovation in our services. He thought it would be a great drawing card, although in those days no "drawing cards" were needed, for everyone that belonged to a church considered it his solemn duty to attend all services. The good elders were horrified at the mere suggestion of such a revolutionary addition to the services. They declared solemnly and most emphatically that if that new-fangled instrument, the "Devil's jewsharp," as they derisively termed the violin, was introduced into our church, they would leave it forever. Of course the "fiddle" was omitted.

But to return to our pioneer dancing parties. Frequently the lone musician had to play all night, as there was usually no one to take his place, and the dancing must go on. But he never seemed to mind it, though he must have grown very weary. There was also always someone in every community that knew how to "call." This was really quite an art, as the caller had to keep his wits about him, else the dancers would become confused and be unable to keep time with the music. Nowadays, this system of "calling" has largely fallen into disuse, but in the distant days, when quadrilles were favorites, it was a large part of the enjoyment of the dance. If the caller did not understand his vocation, much of the swing and symmetry of the dance was lost.

I must tell you about the big flood that occurred while we were living on the Coquille. It was a very disastrous one. The Indians declared that never before in the history of the river had such "big, bad water" been seen. In the winter of 1861-1862 we had some remarkably cold weather and much snow fell in the Coast Range mountains. Soon after the snowfall ceased, a warm Chinook wind set in, blowing steadily for three days. This wind caused the snow to melt rapidly, with the result that every little rivulet, creek and brook was soon overflowing and sending down great volumes of water to the already bank-full Coquille. As a natural consequence the river soon began rising dangerously. It soon overflowed its banks, flooding the lowlands and some of the higher lands. It was a time of terror for us all. We did not know what to expect nor how long the rising waters would continue to overflow the country.

So quickly did the freshet come, bearing everything before it, that the settlers had scant time to protect themselves, their belongings or their stock from the sudden great onrush of flooding waters. No human beings lost their lives in this flood, but an uncounted number of animals perished and much valuable property was destroyed. Fortunately for us, our little home was situated on high ground, beyond the reach of the swift-flowing waters. But our stock did not fare so well as we did. There was little time to round up the cattle, the pigs and chickens and drive them to the higher hills. They were all frightened and difficult to manage. Animals usually get panicky and unmanageable in time of peril. They seem to have an almost uncanny sense of danger at such times.

The family living at the Forks was forced to witness their

home and its contents swept away, and they were powerless to save it or anything that it contained. They had to flee for their lives. Left homeless, they came to stay with us for a few days until they could secure other quarters. Though our cabin was small, we were glad to share it with our unfortunate neighbors and thankful that it was left unharmed.

It was pathetic to see the awful destruction wrought by the merciless flood. The little tannery, owned and operated by some newcomers and located not far from us, was swept away and carried over the bar many, many miles below. Several good log cabins floated past us, each one representing somebody's home, upon which much time and loving labor had been spent. We saw countless cattle, pigs and chickens drifting helplessly down the stream. A number of the settlers whose houses were on low ground, or the bottom lands, took refuge on the roofs of their cabins or in the branches of trees, from which they were rescued with difficulty. They had no time to attempt saving their household goods or flee to the uplands for personal safety. Before the flood, we had eight cows. After it was over we had but three. From some forty or fifty head of hogs we found five left. Most of my big flock of chickens were drowned. Many of our flourishing young fruit trees, planted in the bottom land and which I had cultivated and nourished with great care, were uprooted and washed away.

Fortunately there was no wind during the crest of the flood. Everything was quiet save for the occasional squeal of a frightened pig, the squawk of a drowning chicken or the splash of some big tree as it toppled into the stream. The vast volume of water rolling along, its surface covered with fragments of every imaginable kind, was majestic and terrible in its swift, devastating course.

While the flood was at its height, my husband, Mr. Bottolph and John Dulley took a big canoe and started out across the waste of waters, partly from motives of curiosity and adventure, and also with a desire to be of assistance to anyone in trouble. They paddled down to the lower village below the Forks, finding it entirely under water. Mr. Hall, a settler there, was hurriedly loading his household goods into a big canoe, in the hope of salvaging them. Here the three men found immediate work. They set to with a will, but while they were hastening to get everything out of the cabin before the rapidly advancing waters reached it, the little home floated away while its owners stood dejectedly on the bank and watched it go from them, the labor of many long weeks gone forever—gone through no fault of theirs— leaving them alone and homeless. As there was now no more work for the three visitors to do, they returned to their canoe and paddled across lots and farms in an endeavor to reach Meyersville, where they knew the flood was high. With debris drifting around them and a swift current opposing them, their canoe was soon overturned, and for some time the three adventurous knights were obliged to swim in the icy waters, pushing their clumsy craft before them. Finally they reached Meyersville to find all the near-by settlers assembled there. All the cabins had been washed away and everybody was homeless. A blazing bonfire lent a note of cheerfulness to the sad surroundings and by its warmth the visitors were soon dry and ready for work.

Among those that had lost heavily by the flood was the old German of the Fourth of July celebration, who had prophesied so correctly that there would be "many beobles" there.

Innumerable good logs and boards were constantly drifting by, most of these destined to go over the bar and eventually find lodgment on the ocean beaches where already countless hundreds of logs were piled in shapeless confusion. It seemed a pity to lose all that excellent lumber for which there was now an immediate need; and some of the homeless men actually attempted to save some of it. Among those was our jolly, big-hearted German friend. As he stood on a pile of drift, a long pole in his hands and a short black pipe in his mouth, he suddenly lost his balance and tumbled headlong into the swirling waters. He could not swim, and all felt fear for him, but just as several men were about to leap into the water for him, he re-appeared, still holding his beloved pipe in his mouth and still puffing calmly away at it. Friendly hands were instantly outstretched to him and he was soon warm and dry, none the worse, apparently, for his involuntary bath, and ever after that ready to laugh good-naturedly at the bantering of his friends about his "smoking under water."

The damage done by the flood was a paralyzing blow to the folk on the upper river.As a consequence some of the people were completely discouraged and moved from the river permanently. Others exchanged their farms along the river banks for cattle ranges in the distant hills, feeling that they were safer there. It was really many years before the effects of the great flood ceased to be felt. Even now, old settlers that passed through that dreadful ordeal of danger and destruction, speak of it with reluctance and emotion.

After this disaster my husband seemed to lose all interest in farming on the Coquille. He was completely discouraged. He reasoned that what had happened once might happen again. However, I was inclined to be more hopeful and thought it highly improbable that another such catastrophe would occur in the next hundred years or so. I realized that our place was a fine one. We had done remarkably well in the comparatively short time we had been on the river and had made a good start towards having a splendid farm. It was really little short of a tragedy to have all our hard work destroyed in a few brief hours. It did seem almost hopeless to start practically from the beginning again, but I was willing to do it. I felt the place was worth it. However, I can see now that neither of us felt just the same about going on with the cultivation and improvement of our "claim" after the flood. It had taken the heart out of us.

When we first moved over to the Coquille Valley, we used to see a good many Indians around. As the number of white settlers increased, the natives gradually moved farther back into the interior. The Coquilles, especially those that lived near the coast, had originally been extremely warlike and hostile to the palefaces, but they had been thoroughly chastised in 1851, after their attack and massacre of members of the T'Vault expedition. Later they received even more severe punishment for crimes committed against the white people and they had been well-behaved since then.

About the only time when we saw many natives around was when big celebrations or picnics were held. On these occasions some of the more civilized Indians would appear in the background, hovering on the outskirts of the crowd. They were usually dressed in their picturesque costumes, not yet having acquired the white man's clothing. The women wore their fringed buckskin skirts, with many strings of beads and wampum around their brown necks and arms. The little dark-skinned "papooses" were carried on their mothers' backs in a big basket, the woven strap that held it passing over the squaw's forehead—in the same manner as they carried all burdens. The older children, bright-eyed little creatures, would cling to their mothers' skirts like frightened animals. It seemed to me that Indian children were always extremely shy, or bashful. Apparently they were trained to understand that "children should be seen and not heard." The chief reason that the natives liked to congregate at these big gatherings of the white folks was to gather up the scraps of food that were left.

The pioneers were a generous folk, even if their own allowance was sometimes scanty, and they never begrudged the Indians the "leavings" of a feast. Then, too, the natives liked to watch the white people and copy their ways and manners when convenient.

One of the great events on the river was the arrival of the little schooner *Twin Sisters*, owned and operated by Captain Rackleff. The boat was of about forty tons burden and sailed up from San Francisco whenever possible with a miscellaneous cargo of goods to sell to the settlers. Her small cabin was fitted up like a store, with shelves and counters, and all goods were sold direct from there. It was always an interesting time when the *Twin Sisters* was tied up at her

landing near us. I frequently visited her, not always to purchase things, but oftener out of mere curiosity. It was stimu-
lating to meet the many different people that came and went,
whom we had not seen for months, perhaps, and to watch
the queer current of life that constantly flowed past the little
schooner.

People came from far up and down the river to replenish
their dwindling supplies in every line, all feeling certain that
the *Twin Sisters* could supply their every need.

In 1862 I learned that a Federal law had been enacted
declaring that all public lands might be sold to provide funds
for carrying on the Civil War. As my husband had neglected
to file on our claim, it could have been taken away from us,
bought by someone else, after all the time and money we had
spent on it. My husband was at this time again prospecting
in Idaho. There seemed nothing for me to do but to go to
Roseburg, sixty miles away, where the nearest Land Office
was, and file on our claim myself. It took considerable courage on my part to make this trip under the existing conditions, but I simply had to do it or risk losing our place.
I knew there were people that would have liked to get it.

Fortunately for me, I discovered that two of my neighbors
were in the same predicament regarding their land, so we
arranged to go to Roseburg together. I borrowed Mrs.
Yoakam's old white mare, "Liz"; left my twelve-year-old
daughter in charge of my family of five—I had a darling
little son now—and started out, not without many misgivings. My husband's gun hung in a conspicuous place in the
cabin and I had instructed my little girl how to use it in case
of an emergency, if any wild animal prowled too near the
house and disturbed her. I did not fear either the Indians
or the settlers. I knew the latter would protect my children
and the former were too cowed to commit any depredations.
Nevertheless I did not feel very joyous or light-hearted as
we started on our journey.

Our way led through a beautiful country, with wonderful
dark forests on both sides—fine places for panthers to lurk

in. I never once thought of wild beasts. My mind was full
of my little family and the great adventure upon which I was
embarking. We followed a grassy, overgrown trail most of
the distance, my two companions walking near me, as they
had been unable to procure animals for riding. I was entirely
unaccustomed to riding horseback, and the first time we came
to a fallen log I reined in poor, gentle old Liz too tightly,
and naturally she had to jump over the obstruction instead
of stepping lightly over it, as she would otherwise have done.
As the mare jumped, I fell off, landing on the soft, mossy
grass. Luckily I was not hurt in the least and I learned a
valuable lesson in horseback riding right there. We spent
two days on this journey, stopping at night at "Day's Place"
in Camas Valley.

About twelve or fifteen other travelers were staying there
that night and I was greatly amused and entertained to hear
several "red-hot" discussions and arguments about slavery
and the Civil War. This was all the finest sort of entertainment for me, absent so long from all such matters. The arguments were between a fiery southerner and a still more fiery
abolitionist. The discussion waxed hotter and hotter, the men
were becoming more excited and uncontrollable every moment. Gradually some of the other guests began taking sides.
It looked as though the whole thing might end in a fight
right there and then. Finally one of the excited contestants
challenged the other to "come outside and fight it out!" As
this offer was about to be accepted, mine host of the inn very
emphatically and profanely commanded the combatants to
"quit yer rowin'" on penalty of being compelled to leave the
hostelry. As there was not another stopping place for many
miles, the belligerents were obliged to subside, though they
continued to glare menacingly at each other the rest of the
evening. My young friend, Binger Hermann, was among
those present at the wayside inn that night and he was as
much amused by the heated controversy as I.

At last my two companions and I reached Roseburg. I
must admit that I actually enjoyed myself there. We had

then been living in the wilds of Coos County for nearly nine years and, although I had not been conscious of it, I was positively hungry—starving in fact—for a change of scene and people. Mr. Briggs, the Receiver at the Land Office, was delightfully kind and insisted upon taking me to his home as a guest. While in Roseburg I laid in a stock of useful little articles for the children's coming Christmas and also purchased a few books for them. At that time, however, the supply of suitable books for little people was very limited.

We still have a few of the books that I bought in that distant time, and they are all in fair condition, considering that my six children read and re-read them, and I fancy that some of my grandchildren have also glanced through them. I have forgotten most of the titles, but I remember that one was "A Child's History of England," by Charles Dickens. This was in two small volumes. Dickens wrote this history for his own children when he perceived that they were woefully ignorant concerning their own country's story. These volumes which we have were published by Harper Brothers in 1857 and 1858. Draper's "Chemistry" was another volume I brought home with me. This was mostly for my own use. I also found two or three old Second Readers that I was glad to get for my babies. I was also pleased to find a few French books. This gave me an opportunity to brush up on my favorite language, though I already had several books printed in French.

"Anecdotes for the Young" was another title that I brought back for the children. "Principles Illustrated by Facts," compiled by the Reverend Daniel Smith and published in New York by Lane and Scott in 1852, was still another. People today, and children as well, will smile at these dull titles, as they are entirely different from those we have now. They probably would not be considered very interesting or exciting reading, but my little people enjoyed them amazingly and they also became very familiar with English history, as depicted by Mr. Dickens.

I filed on our land, which I was obliged to take in my own

name, and then we started homeward. Although I had greatly enjoyed my brief outing, I was indeed glad to reach my
little cabin home, for I had worried considerably about the
children. However, I found them all well and happy, not
having missed me in the least, apparently.

It was now October, and the following month my husband
returned from his long prospecting tour, not having had
much success. Naturally he was very busy after his return,
as I had been obliged to neglect many things that really
needed attention. I was especially anxious to have him build
a picket fence around the house so that my chickens could
not bother the flowers I was attempting to grow. But Freeman never seemed to have time for this work. Finally he
succeeded in finding time to dig the post holes and I was
getting ready to do the rest—place the posts and nail on the
boards and the pickets. Just as I was ready to begin this new
work, absolutely new to me, George Cousins arrived from
Empire City with a big bundle under his arm. Several years
before I had made a pair of trousers for him and he had
always declared that they were the most comfortable and
best-fitting ones he had ever worn, so now he had arrived
unheralded, hoping that I would take pity on him and make
him another pair. He was a very large man and could get no
trousers in the country to fit him.

Of course I could not very well refuse to do this small
favor for a man that had walked forty miles to get me to
do it, even if I was a busy woman. George was a carpenter,
so we exchanged jobs—he built the fence and I built the
trousers, using as a pattern an old pair that he had brought
along for that purpose. The result was a very happy one.
In a day or two George had a "brand-new" pair of pants
that pleased him mightily and I had a "brand-new" picket
fence that pleased me quite as much.

I wish it were possible for me to end George Cousins'
history in this light-hearted fashion, but unfortunately I
cannot do so. A few months after his visit to the Coquille,
George went to San Francisco and while there married a

pretty young widow with three small children. Soon after this George, easy-going, good-natured, big-hearted George, embarked on the old brig *Blanco* with his new family, bound for Coos Bay. This was in the winter; storms were many and fierce, and the *Blanco* never reached her intended destination. Months, perhaps a year later, a vague report drifted into Coos Bay that a big ship had come ashore on the beach above the Umpqua, with a number of white people on board. The report said further that the Indians had killed all the persons on the ship, rifled it of its provisions and other things they wanted, then burned the vessel to the sands. This rumor was never verified, and we had no exact means of knowing whether it was true or not. However, many persons were inclined to believe it and thought the unfortunate ship was the lost *Blanco*. It is easy for us to understand how such a story, if true, could gain circulation, even though the natives would attempt to conceal the crime. Many of the white people were very friendly with the Indians; some of the white men had native wives and they could scarcely fail to hear about such an unusual and horrible occurrence.

It was well known that the Umpquas occasionally harbored dangerous criminals—braves that felt an undying hatred for a white man. A wreck like this upon their shores would give them just the opportunity for vengeance that they desired.

Speaking of Indians reminds me of a romance of the forest, with one of its dusky maidens as the heroine. A certain young man of very good family in the state from which he came, settled on a remote claim in the Coquille Valley several years before our advent. All about him was virtually a wilderness, peopled only by Indians. This boy—for such he really was—was a sensible, tactful, kindly young fellow, and by numerous acts of assistance to the natives when they seemed in need of advice from outsiders, he gradually made them all his friends. He had promised his mother before he left his old home that no matter how long he remained among the Indians, he would never take one of them as his wife, even though his life might be very lonely. Now, it happened that the chief of the tribe near which this young man lived, was a good, wise sachem, with one blooming daughter who was the apple of her father's eye.

One day the white lad received a formal visit from this chief. He bore gifts of furs and elk meat. He astonished the young man by telling him that his daughter, the young princess, had given him her love and that she was very unhappy because she feared that her affection was not reciprocated. In his dignified and picturesque language the chief described the sadness of his daughter and his own grief and regret that her choice had not fallen on one of her own people. "The chieftain's heart is warm to the white man," he said. "He would be the friend and brother of the paleface. He would cherish the stranger in his bosom and he would be the great chief's son. Together they would hunt the elk and the deer —together they would smoke the pipe of peace, and together they would discuss the welfare of the tribe about their campfire. The white man holds the heart of the princess in his hand; it is his to keep or to toss away. The chieftain's heart is sad that his daughter looks not upon the young braves of her own people, but the heart of a maiden is like the heart of a bird and flies whither it will."

The white man listened in great embarrassment to the father's story. Then he told him, as gently as possible, of the promise he had made his mother. An Indian is noted for the fidelity with which he keeps a pledge made to his parents and the chief went away sorrowful, for he could not urge the stranger to break his vow. In a short time, however, he came again, renewing his appeal. "Once more I come again to show my heart to the white man," he said, "and it is still heavy. The princess yet dreams of the paleface stranger and grieves that he loves her not. If he takes her to his lodge, he will be of her people. They will follow his counsels and bow their heads before the Great Spirit of his fathers. The chieftain's hands and those of his people are clean—no white man's blood has stained them."

But still the boy felt that he could not conscientiously accept the hand of the Indian girl But few persons are able long to withstand subtle flattery, and such this really was, and almost before he realized it, he began to feel a tender interest in this little aboriginal maid, who was innocent and beautiful, and in whose susceptible heart he had inspired such deep affection. Finally the old father came for the third time, declaring that if the white man still refused to turn his eyes in love towards his daughter, she would cast herself down from the top of a high mountain nearby and thus perish miserably. The boy could hesitate no longer. He realized that if the girl killed herself because of his refusal to marry her, his own life would not long be spared. He thereupon told the father of his desire to make the princess his wife, and shortly after this they were wedded with the usual Indian ceremonies. To all appearances they lived happily together until the end of the chapter. They were somewhat near neighbors of ours and I often saw the young wife who, under her husband's wise guidance, developed into a capable housekeeper and a careful mother. When I first knew them they were the proud parents of a handsome little boy a few months younger than my own son, and I was somewhat chagrined to perceive that this little half-breed was quicker to learn and in some respects more advanced than my own child.

As time went on, it began to seem more and more impracticable for us to continue living on the Coquille. My husband was absent so much of the time, engrossed in mining or in politics, that the care of the family and the farm was left entirely to me, and I was physically unequal to this double burden. Besides, there were no educational advantages for my growing children. As there was no school for them to attend, I was obliged to employ a private teacher at considerable expense and trouble. I found it impossible, with my numerous duties, to teach the children myself.

We had now lived on the Coquille for nearly two and a half years. I forgot to mention that after the flood we enlarged our claim by the purchase of an additional one hundred and sixty acres of land, part of which was adapted for agricultural purposes, the rest being heavily timbered. For this addition we had paid five hundred dollars. We now decided to leave the place and return to Empire City. Several years later my husband sold our entire holdings on the Coquille for the paltry sum of fifteen hundred dollars—four hundred and eighty acres of as fine land as ever lay outdoors. I deeply regretted parting with it at that price, for I realized that it was an exceptionally fine claim and would be valuable some day—as it has proven to be. The town of Myrtle Point stands on it now. When we moved back to Empire City, where we resided for many years, I suppose we could no longer call ourselves "pioneers." Instead, we had become "old settlers."

THE END